KEEPING *My* MIND

Dealing with Life's questions in my Lifetime

ADRIAN PEEL

WESTBOW
PRESS®
A DIVISION OF THOMAS NELSON
& ZONDERVAN

WestBow Press books may be ordered through booksellers or by contacting:

WestBow Press
A Division of Thomas Nelson & Zondervan
1663 Liberty Drive
Bloomington, IN 47403
www.westbowpress.com
1 (866) 928-1240

ISBN: 978-1-5127-3485-0 (sc)
ISBN: 978-1-5127-3486-7 (hc)
ISBN: 978-1-5127-3484-3 (e)

Library of Congress Control Number: 2016904333

Print information available on the last page.

WestBow Press rev. date: 3/24/2016

CONTENTS

I would like to dedicate "Keeping My Mind: Dealing with life's questions in my lifetime" to my family:

My incredible and gracious wife Lucy – thank you for a life of intimate understanding.

My children Daniel and Andrea – in my wildest dreams I did not anticipate the tremendous blessing the two of you would be in my life.

FOREWORD

Life is a journey. This journey takes us on many meandering paths that can lead to feelings of happiness, joy, contentment, satisfaction, peace and fulfillment. But it can also lead to disappointment, discouragement, depression, grief and pain. Every human being at one point or another in life traverses the various paths. Each situation has an effect on the mind. The happy moments in life are just that – happy – and we celebrate the occasion and the moment. But when life's journey takes us through the paths of grief, pain, or emotional and mental turmoil, we need to be able to keep our minds and navigate through these situations.

This book gives some celebrated insight into the life of the author, Adrian Peel. It highlights some of the understanding he has gained about life, and also some of the decisions he has made along the way. There have sometimes been difficult decisions, and every decision made had a price and a consequence. I wouldn't say that every decision was right, but when it was made, he took ownership for it. The result is that Adrian is living an excited and fulfilled life.

At first I felt some apprehension about writing the foreword to this book. It felt like a conflict of interest, because I know the author more intimately than anyone else, and I am biased because we are both vested in our relationship. Yet that is precisely the reason I am best positioned to write this. For over a quarter of a century I have witnessed first hand the way Adrian processes life events and circumstances. I have been there on the front end of decisions, and after the fact when he is living with them. And I see a close correlation between his intentionality and the quality of inner life he has enjoyed over many years. We've recognized that what he has is a pure gift. So, the genuine goal here is to share this gift with as many people as possible, especially those who don't already enjoy the satisfaction of a high quality inner life.

As we ran the first series of seminars using this work, a central premise became very clear: there are very few definitive answers to life's questions. What is presented here is a *way to deal* with the questions, not the *answers* to those questions. It is impossible for someone else to experience happiness on your behalf. For this reason, the process is much more important than the answers that may be implied by Adrian's documented experiences. These answers will not work for many people and personalities. However, the *way* described is a sure way.

Living together the way we do, according to this framework, has been extremely edifying for me. I have disagreed with many things Adrian has wanted to do, and I have turned things in the direction of my own inclination when I've felt strongly enough about them. But that bedrock he has of a solid anchor in Christ, set on the course of a persuasive purpose, has provided our family with an undercarriage of inner security that simply commands our respect and admiration. This has remained true regardless of good or bad circumstances.

I encourage you to read the book with an open mind and with your own life story as the background. Test the concepts and give yourself time and space to evaluate where life is taking you. I think you'll find it worthwhile and, to the extent that this is helpful to you, we will be tremendously blessed.

Lucy Peel
November 2015

INTRODUCTION

A couple of years ago my brother said to me, "You need to write a book on how to raise children". I had never thought about writing on that subject before. "What if people believe what I write and then my children become dysfunctional?" I asked. "That could mean that I've misled people." "At least they'd have a code that has worked to this point," he said. "Most people don't really have anything credible that they follow".

I have reflected on that conversation for a long time. If there's anything that has worked to this point as far as my children are concerned, it is through the grace of God. By the term *grace* I mean *receiving favor without having earned it*. Now I know that this reference to grace can sound clichéd, but the truth is that you don't have to search to find fault with my children or me. So I don't want to set any false expectations that our method always results in children becoming what we want them to be.

As an example, I know of several colleagues who value high profile careers as critical success factors in life. They have invested heavily in their children to set them on this path. Yet the children have not always shared the same values and have sometimes gone down totally different paths, which they may even regret down the road.

More importantly, in addition to not setting false expectations, I don't want to fail to attribute to God what is due to Him when He intervenes in spite of our mistakes and makes our children successful. For all our best intentions, parents make mistakes.

To use the career example, it is not unusual for parents to push their children along a chosen career path because of their preference, rather than an objectively good fit for the child. Yet things can still adjust and work out well for the child with time.

On the other hand, however, I am privileged as a leader in the marketplace, in my church community and as an international speaker, to have interacted intimately with a diverse group of people on life matters. In my experience and in my circle of influence, I find that the individual's handling of life's questions is a more urgent concern than the framework for raising children. For now then, I'll leave that framework to others. Let's work on the subject of "keeping my mind."

I heard someone say, "The human being will do what the human being wants to do. That's why we don't accept any excuses in this business".[1] "How interesting", I thought. I remembered a conversation with a fellow student while I was doing my first degree. There was lots of work and I was having difficulty focusing on the content in order to grasp it. I would track well for some time and then my mind would wander, particularly when I was bored by the topic. My colleague's perspective was simple: sit down and do the work. Read the material, complete the exercises and you'll understand the concepts. I was spending hours sitting down and doing the work and not *getting it*. His comeback was equally simple: then you don't *want* to *get it*.

This conversation is cruel. Minds more acute and seasoned in logic than mine can quickly and easily poke holes in the conclusions. So this is the way I try to think about it – and I've chosen these previous words in this sentence purposefully. If I don't get what is absolutely important to me, I am the one who feels the pain more than anyone else. Therefore, I need to be the one who does the most to get what I want.

But what do I really want? How can I know what I really want when I don't know everything? The truth of the matter – here's another cliché – is that life is a journey. And your quality of life is a function of the value you get from the journey. The things we value have the potential to bring us satisfaction, and these things sometimes evolve. For example, business travel can be very satisfying for a single person, but can become undesirable later in life if it means missing out on time with your family. Your destinations along the way, and up to the final destination, validate the value of life's journey to you, and set you up for the next phases, whether you believe that they'll be there or not.

So, the final state you want to be in is important because it determines the highways you choose to take at life's moments of decision. It also affects your peace with yourself as you navigate the circumstances along the way.

Now, I am somewhat of a cerebral person. I tend to think things through and try to make sense of them without taking my foot off the accelerator of life. This method of logic making at breakneck speed may seem incompatible or even *mind-blowing* to some, but I believe that this process is as applicable to the free spirited or creative individual as it is to me. In fact, it is available to anyone wherever he/she may be on the map of humanity.

This book is intended for anyone who has questions about their life experience that are causing them inner dissatisfaction. Spiritual people, (who believe in meaningful reality beyond the material universe), sometimes face this because they can't make sense of apparent inconsistencies between what they expect from their faith and what they experience in the practical world. Secular people, on the other hand, sometimes face this same type of inner dissatisfaction because external success fails to bring them the type of joy they expect.

I have chosen to use auto-ethnography as the writing method in this book. This is a reflection on my personal experience as I connect my story to wider understandings of the way life works. Therefore, my Christian worldview is central to the book.

However, my emphasis is on the *process*. So, I encourage readers to evaluate the process and models presented, but to insert your own life experience against them for the best benefit.

Here then is the process I have learned and chosen to live by, laid out below as a series of chapters. It keeps my mind and helps me to deal with life's questions as they come up during my lifetime. I think of it as a magnet that draws me, but that does not have ultimate power over me. I can look at it frequently and choose to remain guided by it, or I can be distracted and lose ground, or I can even dump it and fly off somewhere else in my mind. It's my choice. So far, this process has been a good guide for me despite periodic distractions.

Chapter 1 "Find an Anchor for the Mind" is about stabilizing our minds. "For as he thinks in his heart, so is he":[2] you become what you think about. I think that it's important for us to deliberately decide what we believe. We have to *anchor our minds* on something that we can commit to, knowing that it can keep us whole, or feeling complete within ourselves, and steady on our feet. This anchor is not to prevent us from moving, but to prevent us from endless falling without purpose and even against our will.

My personal position is anchored in the God of the Bible and His self-expression in the person of Jesus Christ. This chapter will describe how the anchor gives me thrill and excitement with personal stability in the face of life events.

Chapter 2 "Find a Purpose for your Life" treats a dual topic that is very frustrating to many people, and an enigma to most: we simply don't understand what it means. This is the combination of vision and values. Simply put, my definition of *vision* is what you want to be as a person, and *values* represent the way you're prepared to deal with life circumstances in order to get there. I'll share my experience in grappling with key questions to finally settle on what is most important to me. Along the way, you'll see that there is a price to pay.

Writing this down will be almost therapeutic for me in that it will confirm, yet again, that my life has been worth something even when I don't feel that this is the case. I find that it is easy to develop tunnel vision and become discouraged during the difficulty of a moment, but that keeping a total perspective is often encouraging as it highlights many positive things around us. This writing is a reflection on that for me. For you, it will serve as a jumping off point – or relaunching – into your own experience in this ocean of opportunity.

Chapter 3 "Find a Framework to Guide your Living" is the most tactical piece of this work. I'll give you a simple one page tool that I use to lay out a life cycle, and the compartments that I think are most significant as it unfolds. The life cycle moves along this progression: learning, training, rising, consolidating, legacy, and counsel. The compartments are God, self, family and finances. You'll be able to easily build the story you want your life to be, while looking at the story it has become thus far, and how this has evolved with time. We'll draw on the legacy of others who have gone before us, and who were kind enough to open up their inner lives to the world, so that we could see not only external outcomes but internal developments as well. The key, however, is that this is only a framework. Your life gives it unique life. Unlike a diary, this tool is intended to be brief enough to hold the whole story on one page. At the same time, you can choose to turn it into your own journal if you want to.

Chapter 4 "What does God want from Me?" begins to unpack the life compartments. God is my anchor so He is the title of the first compartment. Your anchor is what must be the title for your first compartment. Only, be satisfied in your own mind that there is nothing else more capable than your anchor to keep you purposeful and hopeful in both good and bad times. Because if your anchor has that preeminent position in your life, you need to know what it requires from you in order for you to get the highest benefit from attaching yourself to it. In other words, what is most important to your anchor so that you can lock into it?

I will share some things that are important to God, and how my skills and interests equip me to make a difference with those things. You will have the chance to think about what points of attachment you must identify, and begin to establish them.

Chapter 5 "Selfless or Selfish?" is the next most important compartment. Once you've decided what you want and what base you're going to stake your life on, it becomes vital that you maintain yourself so that you can actually make the entire journey ahead of you. If you are not in good shape, you will not have the means to help others.

In the air plane safety drill before take off, the cabin crew tell you that, in the event of an emergency, put your own oxygen mask on first before trying to help anyone else, including your child. The real question here then, is where is the pivot line between being selfless in contrast to being selfish? I will lay out some fundamental things that affect longevity and productivity at different life stages, and share some of my own experiences to bring life to the question.

Chapter 6 "What do I Owe my Family?" is the next compartment and I am really in suspense and anticipation as I wonder what it will hold for you. But who is my family? In a sense, family actually evolves with time and I will share both my experience and a Biblical view on how and why this happens.

I think that what I owe my family changes as my family changes. This has been important to me because it has helped me develop a healthy expectation of child rearing, and this is an area where I have seen many people struggle. My goal is that we would learn to figure out the debt we owe to our family, and then pay it, as time demands it. If we are to lose any peace, let it only be to the extent that we willingly refuse to pay what we know we owe. Then, let the remedy back to peace simply be for us to resume payments where we are, for in this "family economy", back payments are often not an option. For example, you can't relive what you deem to be past failures in child rearing, but you can be the right kind of parent going forward.

Chapter 7 "How much Money is Enough?" is intended to do at least two things: (1) Help us understand how important money is and (2) Help us decide what amount of money is needed to fund the first three compartments. Too many people feel guilty about wanting to make money. This is often linked to our limited concept of God and of good and evil, sometimes stemming from the saying, "(the love of) money is the root of all kinds of evil".[3] My hope is that we can develop right thinking about money by simply paying attention to the way things work around us.

I also want to help us to think about money in a way that makes it serve us and not the other way around. If money is not your ultimate anchor, I have some examples of how it has helped to attach people to their anchor. If money is your anchor, I hope you will consider broadening your thinking to realize that you can serve a greater good without having to relinquish your passion for making money.

In the Epilogue and Selected Bibliography I want to acknowledge one more cliché – there is nothing new under the sun.[4] I am writing this text out of my experience, but my experience and perspective have been enriched by countless readings, talks and leaders, most of whom I cannot remember specifically in order to attribute. Therefore, I claim nothing original in this work, and I will give a survey of other material that will serve you well as you choose to pay attention to keeping your mind by dealing with life's questions in your lifetime.

Adrian Peel
January 2015

CHAPTER 1

FIND AN ANCHOR FOR THE MIND

If you will set your mind on God, keep at it and not quit, He
will keep you completely whole and steady on your feet.
- Isaiah 26: 3 (MSG)

Introduction

How much control do you have? Do you have control over when
you will die? Can you prevent your death for as long as you
want to? Can you control the environment, the storms, or the
instinctive behavior of the wild animals? How many people can
you compel to do what you want them to do? How much control
do you really have?

The journey through life can be quite turbulent. Even
though we know this, we still hit unexpected bumps that have
the potential to take the wind out of us. In some cases, we could
have avoided the bumps by paying closer attention to our choices.
In other cases, even in hindsight, there is no way we could have
avoided the bumps.

Since this element of the unexpected is a reality in our lives,
what are the things that would cause you to feel that life was
hopeless if they were to be taken from you? If you had to take these

things and organize them into a list of most to least important, which one or two items would be at the top end of the list?

Now ask yourself, "Who or what has absolute control over the things that are most important to me?"

Then ask yourself this follow-up question: "What would it take to ensure that the one with absolute control keeps what is most important to me safe?"

You see, we often believe in something so fervently that it underpins the mental frame that we live in. For example, the apostle Paul (who wrote a good part of the New Testament in the Bible) initially believed so firmly in his Jewish religious heritage that he was prepared to kill anyone who even appeared to be a threat to it. He viewed life through the lens of the religious law as he had learned it. As a Pharisee, Paul's measure of success against God's "standard" was the extent to which one complied with the letter of the Old Testament Scriptures. Therefore, in order for anyone to come into right standing with God, it was necessary to comply with the details of the Jewish religious law. To corrupt these details was to strike at the heart of Jewish identity and hence to endanger their very survival. This may explain the zeal with which Paul opposed those Jews who were promoting Jesus, a man who had been killed for challenging conventional interpretations of the Old Testament law.

When he realized that a key part of his basis was mistaken, he had to backtrack and change some things he had believed and even killed for. This Jesus, whose message and people he was persecuting, appeared to him and explained that his persecutions were futile because he had mistaken the truth for error. In fact, Jesus said that He had chosen Paul to be a key messenger of the very message he was trying to destroy. Paul was bold and honest enough to reposition his thinking in order to stand on a secure footing.

But the same nature of realization was too much for Judas Iscariot, a man who had spent almost three years as a close friend of Jesus; he ended up taking his own life. When he realized that his betrayal of Jesus Christ to the religious leaders for money was a mistake, he lost all hope. The Bible is not explicit as to his *exact* motivations for betraying Jesus. One view is that he simply wanted money, while another is that he wanted to put Jesus in a position where he had to demonstrate His power so that they could benefit from the recognition. Either way, when it became clear that Jesus was going to be killed, Judas tried to return the money to the religious leaders, claiming that he had betrayed an innocent man. When they refused to take it, he threw the money in the temple and went away to commit suicide. Choosing this alternative suggests that Judas had lost hope. Therefore, the move from one anchor for your mind to another is not a trivial one.

Now imagine Paul, having joined himself to a community of faith that believes Jesus Christ's message, for which he had given up all of his prior life's successes, discovering some of their flaws. He found issues there that hit at the root of what Christ stood for. Racism, hypocrisy and legalism were evident in the ranks of the early leaders of the New Testament church.

Acts 10 gives evidence that racism was present in the early church. When Peter visited the Roman centurion Cornelius, he mentioned that it was an unlawful thing for a Jew to keep company with a non-Jew, yet God had shown him His approval of these people. It was only as a result of repeat visions from God that Peter came to realize that all people are equal in God's eyes, regardless of their race.

However, it was Peter who, after eating with non-Jews, withdrew from them in Antioch when other Jews arrived. Peer pressure caused Peter to try to meet the Jewish stereotype of not eating meals with people of other races. This Galatians 2 story has Paul calling Peter out for his hypocrisy.

Finally, in Acts 15, certain Christian Jews were requiring that non-Jews be circumcised according to the law of Moses as a prerequisite for acceptance into the Christian faith. Paul opposed this vigorously, and this led to the council in Jerusalem, where his motion carried that the burden of Jewish law not be placed on non-Jews who wanted to be Christian.

These types of issues had the potential to cause Paul to step out of this Christian mind-set and into nothingness. To forsake the Jewish worldview he had given his life for, and then to find such dysfunctional thinking in the Christian worldview he had been led to embrace, could have been disconcerting, potentially resulting in disillusionment.

There are people all over the world who are losing their peace of mind for one reason or another. How do you keep your mind when life's questions come at you?

In this chapter, I am addressing a spiritual topic and not a purely medical one. Some people have mental issues that are addressed by medical science and I am not qualified to speak to that. My assignment here is a spiritual one: to uncover a way that God has made for us to keep our peace of mind when life's questions come against us.

What are the deeper life questions that bubble up during times when things go contrary to what we expect? Why does this sometimes cause such turmoil? Denial in all its forms is not an effective response to these questions. This is where we most need an anchor for our minds, one that sustains us.

Before I describe my anchor, please understand that the anchor is not only designed to prevent us from moving, but also to prevent us from endless falling without purpose or even against our will. A certain type of boat anchor will permit the boat to move in its intended direction through stormy waters, but another type of anchor is deep enough to be little affected by the forces at the surface. Likewise, an effective grounding for our minds can enable us to move through the vagaries of life with purpose, peace and steadiness.

In Isaiah 26:3, we read these words: "You will keep him in perfect peace, Whose mind is stayed on You, Because he trusts in You." We can break this verse into three parts from the bottom up and speak of the root, the ground, and the tree's fruit. I will use this to describe how I look at trust in the God of the Bible as the anchor for my mind.

TREE/FRUIT= Perfect Peace
GROUND = Mind stayed on Thee
ROOT = Trust in Thee

Figure 1.1 Tree Diagram.[5]

Find an Anchor to Trust In

The root of the framework is at the end of the verse: "because he trusts in you." My experience is that in order to feel that we're progressing in the right direction, it is important to trust in someone or something.

As I reflect on my development as a person, I find four things that are most important: God's approval, education, the dedicated love of one woman, and money.

I Wanted God's Approval

My mental image of God formed with Him being an authority figure. I do not state this as an evaluation but merely as a fact of the development of my thinking. In my experience growing up from as far back as I can remember, I viewed an authority figure as one with the ability and practice of rewarding acts and attitudes that pleased him or her, and punishing those that did not. While this is a one-sided view of our multifaceted God, it nonetheless was validated in some aspects of God's character as illustrated in the Bible. So the Bible stories I learned as a little boy matched what I read in later years in the Bible. At a general level, God rewards those who do His will and eventually will punish those who oppose His will.

This would explain why I gave up on my chances with God at the age of seven when I told my mother that there was no hope of me going to heaven. No matter how much I tried, I was too naughty and God had given up trying to make me good. In my mind at the time, the only option was punishment.

Amazingly though, I didn't stop trying to do what I thought would please Him. And while there are certainly nonnegotiables in the Bible, I was to learn later of the forgiving and loving nature God has towards me. More importantly, in the heat of every major decision point in my life, I've felt a quiet presence, sometimes even guiding me, which I have learned to trust. In my worldview, this is the presence of God.

I Wanted Education

I was raised to the age of fifteen in a society where racial segregation was legal. It was considered acceptable to deny public facility access to people based on the color of their skin. At the same time, certain privileged ethnic groups had no restrictions, with access to whatever public facilities they wanted.

I remember a time when, as little children, we asked my mother for something to eat. We had walked into a supermarket and stood at a bakery counter waiting to be served. We saw other people come in, get attended to, and leave. After a few minutes, one of the ladies leaned over the counter top and said, "I'm sorry but we don't serve you here".

I have been in the place where someone had the right to walk through a door of opportunity, and I have been openly denied that right because I was not of a particular ethnic group. More than that, I have also experienced denial of opportunities because I belonged to a subset of ethnic groupings. By way of example, before my country's independence I could not attend certain schools because I was not white. After independence, I was blocked from certain positions because I was of mixed race origin, though this was not official law at the time.

However, the benefits that such opportunities offered were not in any way diminished in my mind because of the barriers. And to me, education was the key that held the promise of access to the benefits that the law, or simple prejudices, had locked me out of.

Yet, when my friends and I celebrated my achievement of a First-class degree, and assessment from the Dean that I was among the top fifteen students in the history of the Faculty of Engineering, my good friend remarked, "What's wrong with you? It seems like we are happier about your success than you are."

The truth is that I am both grateful and glad for my education. It has opened outer doors that would otherwise have remained shut. It just didn't open inner doors within me. Education didn't bring me any more of the deep contentment I wanted, but was something of an anticlimax in that regard.

I Wanted the Dedicated Love of One Woman

I'm not certain, but I think that my desire for the dedicated love of one woman was all about respect. To this point, I do not have the logic to explain why this is the case, but I resonate intuitively with the statement. I am blessed with a lovely wife in mind, spirit and body, but I learned the limitations of a relationship with a woman to secure that respect before I met my wife. Through a series of relationships prior to meeting my wife, I discovered that for various reasons women were not enough to satisfy my need for respect, and I knew that the need was deep.

I now understand more clearly that all people are imperfect and that we make mistakes. The level of acceptance and commitment that I expect is a standard that is humanly unreasonable to attain. So, as much as I cherish the dedicated love I share with my wife, I know that it cannot be the anchor I referred to earlier.

I Wanted Money

The media and images that people project gave me an early impression that those with money have control over their own destinies. In my case, corporate executives looked like they had achieved such a station in life. So I researched it, talked to people about it, and worked very hard to get there. I was very fortunate to get onto the senior management track of a major multinational corporation at a very young age in my career. I reached my target level of responsibility and income within a decade of leaving university.

Strangely enough, I had lots of disposable income but very little discretionary time. I was also under the control of "powerful" superiors, some of whom ended up getting fired – something of a contradiction to me. So I had the money but I didn't have the control.

As I write this chapter, in the fiftieth year of my life, the only important factor that has been unyieldingly consistent in giving me peace is that quiet presence. This is not to say that the other three factors are no longer important to me: they still are. But this is to say that none of those three have been able to satisfy my inner need in the solid way that God has.

The Man who found the Treasure he Wanted

In Matthew 13: 44 Jesus compares the kingdom of heaven to a man who finds treasure in a field, then goes and sells all he has in order to buy the field. He trusts the treasure, believing that it will meet all his needs. This is why he can sell off everything else – because he doesn't believe that those other things have what he needs, otherwise he would have kept them.

Because he has placed his trust in the treasure, he has exposed his most vulnerable parts – his heart and his future for example – to this treasure, and it will impart into his innermost being what it has to offer. If what the treasure offers is good, it will build confidence and passion because by definition treasure has the capacity to enrich. But if it is bad, it will break down into confusion because the "enrichment" it brings is unexpected, undesired and not what the man was trusting for. If the man has nothing else to trust in, he'll lose his mind on account of the broken confidence.

When there's nothing left to trust in, people lose their hope and invariably lose their peace of mind. And in their confusion, adversarial forces take charge in their minds. Then people begin to do strange things regardless of their station in life.

Because what they have trusted in has failed them, in their minds some people go into a *free fall* grasping for stability but being suspicious of any thing they happen to grab a hold of. It's tantamount to yet another cliché – a drowning man grasping at straw – except in this case, the drowning man knows that the straw is debris and not a symbol of hope.

We all need a solid, dependable anchor for our minds. For me, I have chosen to trust God and accept Him as my anchor. What does that mean in terms of what I choose to do? This takes us to the second part of Isaiah 23: 3, which holds the root of what we trust.

Commit your Mind to the Anchor you Trust

The *ground* of the model is in the middle of the verse: "whose mind is stayed on you". If we want to get the benefits from the person or thing we've chosen to trust, we need to lock into it. Your mind is akin to the ground, and the root is the anchor you trust in.

Many studies of successful professionals find that while natural gifting in a certain area is an unquestionable advantage, it is neither necessary nor sufficient for success. Practice is more of a factor than innate ability is.

Think about something that you have distinguished yourself in, perhaps something that others would gladly entrust to you. How much time have you spent doing this over the course of your life, even as a hobby? People usually distinguish themselves after spending time and paying attention to their area of interest.

Now think about something you had a sparkle for in your younger years but did not spent much time on. How much of an expert are you in that space today? Many of us have stories of what might have been had we paid more attention to certain areas we feel are natural giftings. My observation is that time and focused attention make a big difference to the level of success we enjoy in any given area.

You need to Practice if you're going to Win

As a teen I competed in athletics at a provincial level. As our schools became integrated with the coming of political independence in 1980 to the country I grew up in, the competitive landscape opened up.

I had a friend who had a natural talent for long distance running. In the 1500m race, he beat the reigning junior provincial champion by coming in first place. The following year he didn't take the track meet seriously. He was dispassionate and puberty was striding forward. Before the race he smoked his cigarette, came out to the starting line and did a few stretches. My friend had demonstrated that he had talent, but he failed to nurture that talent through practice. Furthermore, he didn't prepare his mind and body leading up to the competition, not recognizing that building up to peak performance is usually intentional. His rival was warmed up, ready and purposeful after a year of serious preparation. The opponent won the race convincingly and my friend never regained that top position. He was good but his talent worked for him once. Dedicated practice worked for his rival each year after that to the end of his high school career.

"For as he thinks in his heart, so is he" (Proverbs 23: 7): you become what you think about. I think that it's important for us to deliberately decide what we believe. We have to anchor our mind on something that we can commit to, knowing that it can keep us whole and steady on our feet. Then we spend time with what we've committed to: this is *practice* for the mind.

Jesus brings Eternal Power to the Present by God's Word

Hebrews 6: 19 describes the hope we have in Jesus, "as an anchor of the soul, both sure and steadfast, and which enters the presence behind the veil." Through Jesus, who has "passed the veil" of death, we who believe in Him and have a relationship with Him can access hope from eternity so that it is active in our earthly lives.

Verse 17 speaks of the immutability or unchanging nature of God's counsel, which He wants to show to the heirs of His promise. God's advice to us doesn't change. The timing may be different, but the essence is the same. However, it only works for us if we commit to Him, which makes us eligible to appropriate the things He has promised. How will He show us His advice, bringing a perspective from eternity into the domain of time? Through His Word – the Bible – which enters us through our minds.

And if we sell out to His Word, then our minds become locked into Him, or settled on Him. Fastened to this rock, which cannot move[6], we become immoveable and will keep our minds when the storms come, whether or not we understand what is going on around us.

This is why Jesus, when He was being tempted in the desert, kept bringing the conversation back to the Word of God. The purpose of the temptation was to distract Him from His mission to give his life so that humanity could be saved. Jesus had gone to the desert to fast from food and everyday activities and to focus on this mission when the distractions came. Even though the circumstances created a crisis within Him for food, fame and influence, He kept His mind *stayed* exclusively on the Word of God. Because He trusted that all He needed as a man was available to Him in God.

Enjoy Peace through your Commitment to your Anchor

Finally, the root of trust anchors the mind, so that the tree delivers the fruit of peace. "You will keep him in perfect peace, Whose mind is stayed on You, Because he trusts in You." (Isaiah 26:3)

The tree's fruit is at the front of the verse. It is essential to be sure that what we have put our trust in is able to give us the benefits we're looking for. I have noticed that inner peace is the primary benefit I am looking for regardless of whether the circumstances around me are good or bad. By inference then, this must be found beyond the material and in the eternal world.

In Colossians 1: 27 Paul says, "Christ in you [is] the hope of glory." As Christians the seat of our souls is Jesus Christ. This is because our deepest needs have been satisfied by His peace that surpasses all understanding. This is why we love God with all of our heart, *mind,* soul and strength. I read the Bible and think about what God says and how it applies to my life, and then I try to live this out everyday. It informs the way I choose to respond to situations.

My Peace is Christ's Expression
to *Me* and to *Others*

A thought that I find important is the fact that the fruit is essentially the expression of the tree. In fact, the fruit is the part of the tree that allows it to duplicate itself. The fruit is the tree in another form, but the tree does not eat the fruit. Looking at it from a different perspective, the tree is the fruit's way of reproducing itself. From either point of view, the image is that Christ's peace finds its expression in us through His Word. The tree produces the fruit to replicate itself, and for *others* to feed on and enjoy it. Excess fruit may die and with time be recycled through the soil and into the tree again but that is a subsidiary and less efficient function.

The peace that I have as a result of being anchored in Christ is something for me to experience in my very core, inasmuch as I am an extension of Him. He put it this way in the Bible, "I am the vine, you are the branches". (John 15: 5) Yet there are others who will come and eat the fruit of the peace that I have – men, women, rich, poor, old, young and so on. So my peace is also on open display for others to come and enjoy it.

Here's another thought: could it be that in order for me to keep my peace, I need to give it away? I think I understood this to be the case a long time ago, but the concept didn't seem to fit in the world we live in. I have found that trying to be at peace with everyone in the corporate world can *seem* to be a liability on several fronts. The reality though, is that taking the less travelled path of truly dignifying people even when there appears to be no gain for you, leads to deeper long-term impact. So, I am learning how to be able to get results while still elevating the worth of individuals in my own mind, even when I have to go up against them in various matters. May God help me to remain gracious at all times and in all situations and represent His principles well.

Does this Really Work for Me?

The conclusion I have come to so far in my life has led me to face my days with tremendous optimism. Whatever external failures I have had, I always feel that I am on the edge of something great. I am excited by the possibility that someone might be inspired enough by something I do or say that would cause them to positively impact the lives of others around them. It thrills me to see people excel beyond what they expected they could do. But my steadfast approach to this life stands on the expectation I have of one day hearing the authority figure – God – say to me, "Well done good and faithful servant…enter into the joy of your Lord."[7]

Conclusion

People have yearned for food as children in poor lands, but found that it wasn't enough once they had it.

People have craved fame and given their lives to achieve it, but found that it wasn't enough once they had it.

People have desired power and influence, but found that it wasn't enough once they had it.

These things can all be good, but they are temporary and therefore moveable. In my opinion, only God can give you perfect peace, because only He is eternal and therefore immoveable.

I have chosen to place my trust in God and to anchor my mind in His Word. He keeps my mind and has caused me to deal adequately with life's questions during my lifetime so far. I read His Word and think with the goal that it should form me, so that it becomes my response to every question life brings. Then, I live in perfect peace in spite of the vagaries of this life. "And the peace of God, which surpasses all understanding, will guard your hearts and minds through Christ Jesus." (Philippians 4:7)

Now it's back to you for a time to reflect on my earlier questions. What are the things that, if they were to be taken from you, would cause you to feel that life was hopeless? If you had to take these things and organize them into a list of most to least important, which one or two items would be at the top end of the list?

Here's the next question: "Who or what has absolute control over the things that are most important to me?"

Then ask, "What would it take to ensure that the one with absolute control keeps what is most important to me safe?

Take some time to jot down some answers before you go to the next chapter.

CHAPTER 2

FIND A PURPOSE FOR YOUR LIFE

Where there is no vision the people are unrestrained.
- Proverbs 29: 18 (NASB)

For which of you, intending to build a tower, does not sit
down first and count the cost, whether he has enough to
finish it — lest, after he has laid the foundation, and is not
able to finish, all who see it begin to mock him, saying,
'This man began to build and was not able to finish'?
- Luke 14: 28 – 30

Introduction

There are some things we accomplish as we move through life
that give us a tremendous sense of meaning. I have enjoyed seeing
the deep look of satisfaction on the face of a mechanic when
the engine he had been struggling with for hours, roared to life
after a mechanical crank. I have had the pleasure of watching an
old colleague trying to contain his pleasure as he recounted the
degrees his four children received and the prestigious positions
they now hold.

In times like these I frequently ask myself what is at the heart of this satisfaction. After reaching some of my earliest accomplishments, I became acquainted with the idea of the anticlimax. This happens when we anticipate something with euphoric experience. When we accomplish the feat, it not only doesn't quite meet what we expected, but more significantly, doesn't continue beyond the moment. It's like climbing to the peak of a tough hill and then suddenly finding yourself descending down the other side.

For those who can't relate to the short "high" of the mountain top experience, consider the institution of marriage, and the "great expectation" of the literal union. My wife Lucy and I were fortunate to have very good pre-marital counseling. The Pastor, obviously among many other things, cautioned us that the consummation of the marriage was not everything that people made it out to be. Without question the experience would be great, but he wanted to manage our expectations. I am thankful for the pragmatism that he brought to me in this area.

Very early in my twenties I began to seriously question the purpose of my existence. I quickly came to the conclusion that I must have been created to serve God in full time ministry in the church and that this would give me the ongoing sense of meaning I was looking for. I had already been recommended for ministry preparation as a Christian brother and then as a Catholic priest. In each case I got *cold feet* in the twilight moments. But after I experienced the anticlimax associated with achieving one of the highest results in my first degree in engineering, I decided that I was going to Bible school and dedicating myself once and for all to full time ministry.

Then I had a remarkable encounter with God. He impressed upon me through the life of Moses that He actually wanted me to thrive in the secular environment. I felt Him say that we would revisit my desire to enter full time ministry at the age of forty. So I burst out of the starting blocks in pursuit of my corporate career.

Thus began my really earnest pursuit after purpose. I will outline this journey, not entirely in chronological order, but in the sequence that now makes sense to me looking back. The reason for this approach is that I often did not understand what I was going through, but subsequently learned the language to explain or make sense of some of it after the fact.

There's one more reference I want to offer before getting into the *weeds* of this topic. It is called Maslow's hierarchy of needs[8]. This theory seeks to describe what motivates people. It says that we all begin at the bottom of the following pyramid and ascend the rungs until we get to the apex. It helped my understanding as life unfolded.

The most basic of human needs is *physiological*. People are motivated to access the things that support physical survival. This includes things like air, water, food and sleep. When these elements are scarce they become the dominant quest of a human being. Bars of gold are of little significance to someone who is dying of thirst.

Where physiological needs are relatively provided for, Maslow proposed that people tend to prioritize *safety* needs. This is where aversion to personal, financial and health risks become more evident. Security of dwelling, employment and exposure to disease cause us to take steps to mitigate such risks. Insurance policies and savings accounts are examples of tools provided to accommodate this motivation to be safe.

With physiological and safety needs attended to, Maslow saw *love and belonging* as the next motivation for people. People desire community and are motivated by the need for acceptance by others. The group can be small or large but the mutual sense of exchanging love by both giving and receiving it is a basic human need. The theory goes so far as to include sexual intimacy in this category.

Beyond this comes the need for *esteem*. With physiological, safety and community needs met, the motivation for respect of both other people and self comes to the fore. The word "independence" is a good word to describe this level. It is related to people developing an authentic sense of worth.

Finally, *self-actualization* is positioned at the top of Maslow's hierarchy of needs. At this level, people are motivated to become the best they can be. The word "best" in this context is subjective in the sense that one's capacity and the standard for performance is driven more by internal satisfaction than by purely external assessments. Here, for example, people accept facts more readily, are more creative and tend to lack prejudice.

It is important to note that Maslow acknowledged that boundary lines are blurred between the levels and that multiple needs can be in play at the same time while also changing with time.

An outcome of Maslow's model could be that our purpose changes as we move through his five phases. My approach, however, is to view purpose as a single overarching life "calling". I am defining "purpose" as the combination of "vision" and "values". Let's go into a definition of vision and values as it pertains to this discussion.

Vision

I am defining "vision" as what you want to be as a person. It is formed out of two interconnected states: the way things ought to be, and the way things are.

Bill Hybels, the founding and senior Pastor of Willow Creek Community Church in South Barrington, Illinois, uses the terminology "Holy Discontent" to describe our dissatisfaction with the way things are. This is a current reality that really rubs us the wrong way. We see conditions and connect them with a problematic state of affairs. And we feel within our core that this is wrong and it doesn't need to be that way. Every time we see this particular situation, our level of dissatisfaction with it grows. There are generally three basic responses to what we feel: run away from the situation, live with the pain, or have enough of it and decide to change it. This third response is what leads to the way things ought to be.

When we begin to see clearly that the situation can be changed to eliminate the things that are irking us, vision is beginning to form. Martin Luther King Junior's "I have a dream" speech is an incredible encapsulation of this framework. King was an American civil rights leader who was assassinated in the late 1960s. He envisioned American society without racism, where people would be judged by the content of their character rather than the color of their skin. He delivered this vision publicly and very effectively in his speech at a time when people were being killed for this cause. To the extent that we can articulate a compelling future state that deals with the issues of our holy discontent, we can say that we have a vision, in my opinion. So how did this flow out in my experience?

From as far back as I can remember, I have always felt an internal indignation rise up when I saw anything that I perceived to be injustice. Let me describe a case in point. In high school I had two colleagues I will name Shane and Ben. Ben was a little bigger than Shane physically, but they were in the same class and were almost always together. Shane could never seem to have enough good things to say about Ben, both in and out of his presence. They were often together at recess and were evidently very good friends. At the back of my mind I didn't miss the fact that even though they related well to each other, Ben never said anything good about Shane. He didn't say anything bad that I was aware of, but there just seemed to be an imbalance between Shane's good words about Ben, and Ben's relative silence about Shane.

One day as we were at recess a noisy commotion suddenly broke out, and as the crowd of boys parted, there were Ben and Shane, physically fighting. Ben overpowered Shane. The fight was stopped and even though he was red faced and flustered, Shane's priority was to shake Ben's hand and apologize to him.

At the end of the school day I bumped into Ben as we went to get the bus. Before I had time to think I found myself reprimanding Ben for the fact that Shane had always held him in such high regard and asking how he could humiliate such a person the way he had done at recess. I can still see Ben backing away saying, "I already told him I'm sorry". I didn't know what had started the fight in the first place. I just felt the intuitive sense of a lack of equity, of injustice at play.

My intuitive and risky response was cause for reflection because it wasn't the first and would not be the last response of its kind.

On the other side of the coin, I found myself to be an optimist for other people. In particular, I always felt that if I could do something, anybody else could do the same. An example will help.

My older brother (by two years) didn't get the top grades at school. I remember the year that he wrote his first public exams – "O" Level or General Certificate of Education Ordinary Level Examination offered by the Associated Examining Board in England. They had about one week's study leave before the first exam. In the afternoon I would come home from school and find my brother "studying" with his friend. I would overhear them talk about the topics that, if they came up on the exam, would surely result in their failure. This talk was extensive. It covered a wide range of topics and continued for hours. Finally, I went into the room after a few days and said, "Guys, why don't you spend the time learning the topics you don't yet understand rather than wasting time planning your failure on their account if they come up in the exam?"

My brother was able to pass his exams and left school. Some years later when I was doing well at university, I was sitting with my brother and chatting. Apparently I said to him, "You're university material". That statement seems to have changed his self-image and he began to study for his first degree as a mature student. As I write this, my brother has a Doctorate in Business Administration and is enjoying himself as he solves problems for a leading global company.

While I hated injustice, it gradually became visible to me that I loved to encourage people. But I would feel particularly confused when I was misunderstood. Especially as I entered the workforce, I began to find increasingly that some people mistrusted my intentions. A case in point was when I was doing part of my professional engineering training at a workshop for repairing electric motor windings. The engineer in charge asked me to move to my next assignment a week ahead of schedule. I virtually begged him to allow me to finish my task first, even though the move was a positive acknowledgement of my progress. I felt that it would be a personal demonstration of respect if I were to complete the task under the particular artisan, and to do it well. In the future, I could genuinely say that I valued the work that the artisans did. The engineer in charge quietly investigated me because he thought that I wanted to finish the particular job because it was a personal job that I was using company resources to do.

That type of mistrust was hurtful because I didn't want self-gain when it came to these two areas of justice and encouragement. The equilibrium of both justice and a fair attribution of peoples' capability released a destiny type tension within me and that was what was most important. I always felt that I could get the gain that I wanted on the strength of the attributes God had given to me, and that I didn't need to take away from, or not give to, someone in order to get ahead.

To be clear, this is not an indictment on anybody else. Rather, I think that this is part of the growth pain involved in deciphering God's call in my own life. So what did the Bible have to say about this?

During my four years at seminary part time, I was searching for meaning for my life contribution. Through a series of readings, discussions, study and reflection, God led me to rest on Genesis 1: 26 – 28. These verses deal with the fact that God created humanity in His image. This meant that humanity was to be fruitful, multiply and replenish the earth, and to subdue and have dominion over everything God had created in the animal and plant world and indeed over the whole earth. The only part of God's creation that humanity was not given dominion over was other people. I was excited to see reverberations of this theme in different constitutions such as Canada's Human Rights Code, and the American Declaration of Independence statement that guarantees everyone "the inalienable right to life, liberty and the pursuit of happiness".

So my life vision gradually settled deep within my spirit: to recognize the image of God in every person I meet. I want to be a part of helping individuals to open up to the potential God has placed in them, and to be a champion for removal of obstacles placed in peoples' lives, particularly by others who seek to control them with ulterior and selfish motives.

But how does one accomplish this? For one thing, my experience has been that, especially in a capitalist society, the more you try to lift people up, the further you sometimes seem to sink into the ground. Note that providing an economic service or product that is in demand is the exception here. Furthermore, when you need some of the encouragement you give, it can sometimes feel like there is nowhere to get it from. Granted that this may just be perception, but in the spirit of transparency this is something that occasionally does come up. So how am I to deal with life's circumstances in order to get to the vision? Let's move on to the topic of values.

Values

I am defining "values" as the way you are prepared to behave in order to become what you want to be.

The Book of Ecclesiastes in the Bible is a priceless view of life through the experience of a "successful" human being in the twilight years of his life. Many schools believe that the writer of this Book was King Solomon in whose reign the nation of Israel saw the zenith of its secular prominence. To me this brings a certain secular credibility to his observations and conclusions, given that these are centered primarily on the material world we live in. Solomon describes his own pursuit of meaning in the writings of Ecclesiastes. He considers such things as the relentless routine with which the days tick over from generation to generation, of the labor people go through in building on the earth's resources (subduing the earth and having dominion, if you will), of indulging in wine in order to find happiness, and so forth. The book takes almost a despairing tone before it ascends to this conclusion: "Fear God and keep His commandments, for this is man's all". (Ecclesiastes 12: 13)

While I'm in the Biblical mode let me expound one meaning of Solomon's conclusion before I return to its application to my own experience.

The meaning of "fear God" is explicitly described in Psalm 34: 11 – 14. These are King David's words and he is instructing his children. Let us remember that Solomon was one of David's children. The Bible reads as follows:

"Come, you children, listen to me; I will teach you the fear of the Lord. Who is the man who desires life, And loves many days, that he may see good? Keep your tongue from evil, And your lips from speaking deceit. Depart from evil and do good; Seek peace and pursue it."

This is phenomenal insight to me. To use my own words, if I want to live out a meaningful life I need to be pure in what I say, do and think about other people because that is what demonstrates that I fear God. John the Apostle put another spin on it when He said, "If someone says, 'I love God,' and hates his brother, he is a liar; for he who does not love his brother whom he has seen, how can he love God whom he has not seen?" (1 John 4: 20) Thus far, therefore, it seems that purpose lies in who I am *before* or *ahead of* the things I do.

When Solomon described the second duty of man as keeping God's commandments, he would have understood these to be in the law of Moses, or the first five books of the Bible. The rest of the Bible had not yet been written as far as we know. Now Jesus took the Mosaic law and transcribed it into its application in the Age of Grace in which we live. The Sermon on the Mount in Matthew 5 – 7 takes principles of the Mosaic law and applies it to the law of the transformed heart: from what you should do to what you should be. I will extract a few conclusions Jesus presents in this regard.

"Let your light so shine before men that they may see your good works, and glorify your Father in heaven". (5: 16) In my own words, the way you are should cause people to look at what you do and in this acknowledge that God is working through you. It is possible to do something good but with a bad attitude. There's the story of three men in a pit molding bricks. When asked what they're doing, the first man says that he's molding bricks because it's his job. The second man says he's molding bricks because he wants to provide for his family. The third man says he's molding bricks because he's building a magnificent cathedral. There's just something about the third man's answer that inspires me, even though the first two answers are valid. All three may be doing the same work, but their lights are shining differently.

"For I say to you, that unless your righteousness exceeds the righteousness of the scribes and Pharisees, you will by no means enter the kingdom of heaven". (5: 20) The scribes and Pharisees were focused on abiding by the *letter* of the law while Jesus was promoting the *spirit* of the law. Therefore, according to Jesus, your intention is *more* important than your action, without implying that action is *not* important. I've heard the saying that the road to hell is paved with good intentions. The idea is that intentions without actions don't change anything. Yet I would not trust the "good" deeds of someone if I knew that they had malicious intent. At the same time, I continue to trust people who have made mistakes if I know that they meant well. God is concerned about what is behind our actions. It is important, therefore, to keep the source of our motivations pure.

"Therefore you shall be perfect, just as your Father in heaven is perfect. (5: 48) In the context of this discussion, Jesus explains that God provides for both the evil and the good people. What this meant to me is that I should not hold back dignity and respect from any person: period. Like anybody else I have my biases and preferences so acting this out daily is more easily said than done. I am working towards this ideal, painfully aware that I have a long way to go. That said, this settled my occasional lack of reciprocation issue around encouragement from outside. (See the last stanza on the section dealing with vision). I understand that my responsibility is to do what I know is right, and this does not depend on what other people choose to do.

"Therefore do not worry, saying, 'What shall we eat?' or 'What shall we drink?' or 'What shall we wear?'. But seek first the kingdom of God and His righteousness, and all these things shall be added to you". (6: 31, 33) To me this means that my focus should be on *being* what's right in my motivations rather than *having* what's right. I've heard people talk about some things being simple but not easy. This is one of those concepts. Not "worrying" does not mean not "working." Seeking the kingdom of God brings with it a lot of work. The pulse of these conclusions, however, is Jesus' emphasis on godly motivations.

"Do not give what is holy to the dogs; nor cast your pearls before swine, lest they trample them under their feet, and turn and tear you in pieces". (7: 6) In respecting other people, I must remember to respect myself and not put myself into a position where my good can be evil spoken of. Self-awareness is critically important in this regard. I have had to continually remind myself of who I am and what is important to me. Then I find it equally important to intentionally gain an understanding of the culture and objectives of the environment I am in. I am a Christian at church and at work. Empathy and compassion are my best witness of who I am at church. At work, it's integrity and results that do most of the "talking". In my experience, these two witnesses are not always interchangeable between the contexts, even though they are all good attributes.

"Therefore, whatever you want men to do to you, do also to them, for this is the Law and the Prophets". (7: 12) This is also commonly known as the golden rule. Humorously here, I am not talking about the golden rule that states that he who has the gold makes the rules. This is about putting yourself in the other person's place before deciding how to treat them. A caution is that not everything I want may be good for me. For example, I may want to be spared the consequences of wrong doing when that would be bad for me, for God disciplines His own people. Likewise, I must be prepared to make the hard decisions regarding others when it is the right thing to do.

The difficulty for me has always been in finding the right balance between mercy and discipline. To be clear, discipline is not the same thing as punishment or abuse, although I find that the lines have been blurred between the meanings of these words. Discipline is about accountability and consequences. Privileges are withdrawn or restrictions applied in order to motivate acceptable expected behaviors.

At times I have been torn inside while disciplining my children. And yet I have to believe that as long as my heart is continually right before God, those involved will somehow see God's hand in what I am trying to do at a particular point in time. This after all is the essence of the Sermon on the Mount. And if they don't see it, God certainly does.

The extension of these principles to the work place was a challenge to me for a very long time. Many people told me that they are incompatible with the core objectives and philosophy of business, especially in a capitalist model. Resolution came for me when I took a strategy program (the Value Profit Chain) at Harvard Business School. I will summarize what I gleaned from its essence because it was indeed compatible with my values.

The Value Profit Chain derives from an earlier version of work called the Service Profit Chain, which posits that profitable growth comes through customer and employee loyalty.

Loyal employees will stay longer with a company, refer the company to their associates (who often share their values and so come to be loyal employees too), and share their ideas for improvements willingly and enthusiastically. We can create loyal employees by being clear about expectations, training them to be competent, giving them input into decisions that affect them, giving them the tools and resources to do their jobs, and recognizing their contributions. Such employees are most likely to deliver customer satisfaction, which leads to loyal customers.

Loyal customers will continue to purchase the company's products or services, refer the company to others, and tend to buy more of what they need from the company rather than from elsewhere. We can create loyal customers by understanding their needs, working with them to discover the best solutions, involving them in any changes affecting them, and recovering spectacularly when we let them down by not meeting their expectations. Such customers are most likely to contribute to profitable growth because the cost of serving them and of advertising to their associates is reduced when they are "apostles" for the company and actively promoting it.

To me, this was a significantly different approach to business than the cold profit motive. The end game is still to make a profit, but coming at it this way creates an environment that edifies the people, which in turn draws in the profit. It fits with my aspiration of bringing out the best in people I meet, but with purity of intention in my heart.

The reality, however, is that some people only seem to respond to a hard external hand and there is still some dissonance in my mind as to how to address this. I do, however, want to share an insight from King David in his last words. (2 Samuel 23: 3, 6 – 7)

"The God of Israel said, The Rock of Israel spoke to me: 'He who rules over men must be just, Ruling in the fear of God". (3)

"But the sons of rebellion shall all be as thorns thrust away, Because they cannot be taken with hands. But the man who touches them Must be armed with iron and the shaft of a spear, And they shall be utterly burned with fire in their place.". (6 – 7)

I don't know that we ever arrive at the place where we have all of this figured out in this lifetime. Yet my own experience is that fulfillment comes with knowing that I am "chasing after God" and trying to do what I believe He expects of me in every situation, with the right heart attitude. Once again, I need His grace because I fall short.

Conclusion

Wrapping my position up then, I believe that God created me to encourage the best in people who come under my influence, so that they can achieve all their potential while in this world. To the extent to which I pursue His glory in this rather than my gain, I will experience a sense of purpose in this life and God's approval in eternity.

Now, what does this mean for you? I would encourage you to consider the following questions over the coming months. Treat them seriously and they will reward you in kind. We begin with "vision".

1. What is your holy discontent? What do you deeply feel is not as it should be?
2. How can you "be the change that you want to see"?
3. What does your "anchor" from chapter 1 think or say about this?

Write down the answers to these three questions and then read them every night before you go to bed for twenty one consecutive days, which is said to be the amount of time required for a habit to form. I have not found any empirical evidence to validate the claim of twenty one days, but the exact number of days you choose is not critical. What is most important is that you keep at this for long enough to bring the answers to the forefront of your thinking. Use a blank sheet of paper with lots of space, even if you write down very little. As you read daily through what you've written, make alterations when adjustments to what you had written down come to mind. It doesn't need to be tidy: feel free to simply cross things out and make inserts where space permits. Then rewrite what you've come up with on a fresh page and discuss it with someone who you respect and can trust because they are not only confidential but also competent in the things you have written down. This will set you on the path to discover God's vision for your life, but it will likely take much more time and work before you feel a firm sense of what that is.

Now we move to questions around "values".

1. What are five things you are prepared to do in order to become the person you believe God has created you to be?
2. What are you prepared to give up in order to become the person you believe God has created you to be?
3. What does your "anchor" from chapter 1 say or think about this?

Again, write down the answers to these three questions and then read them every night before you go to bed for the next twenty one consecutive days following your vision exercise. Use a blank sheet of paper with lots of space, even if you write down very little. As you read through what you've written daily, make alterations when adjustments to what you had written down come to mind. It doesn't need to be tidy: feel free to simply cross things out and make inserts where space permits. Then rewrite what you've come up with on a fresh page and discuss it with the same person you discussed your vision with. This will set you on the path to discover God's values for your life, but it will likely take much more time and work before you feel a firm sense of what they are.

As you continue down this path of reflection, you will likely experience times where you are not sure that you're on the right track. It would even be normal for you to put the exercise aside for periods of time. But as you seek God and allow Him to take you where you don't know to go, the cloud begins to form into a figure that eventually becomes recognizable. You can then merge your vision and values into a life purpose and allow the *Potter* to perfect it as you pursue Him.

I think a closing thought to this chapter is vital. Please take care to live your life moment by moment during this journey. While our nature is to want to get to the answer, it is most important to develop our relationships with God and others along the way. That is where fulfillment is truly found. To consolidate this thought by way of example, read the story of Martha and Mary found in Luke 10: 38 – 42. Yes, you do need to find a Bible because I'm not re-telling the story here.

CHAPTER 3

FIND A FRAMEWORK TO GUIDE YOUR LIVING

To every thing there is a season, A time
for every purpose under heaven.
– Ecclesiastes 3: 1

Remember now your Creator in the days of your youth,
Before the difficult days come, and the years draw
near when you say, "I have no pleasure in them."
– Ecclesiastes 12: 1

Introduction

Chapter 3 "Find a Framework to Guide your Living" is the most tactical piece of this series of topics. We use a simple Excel based tool to put together a road map for your life. The key to this road map over time is that it is dynamic. Its role is not deterministic but rather it is a guide. Our focus is on three elements: Life cycle, legacy definition and completing the framework.

The term "life cycle" is a commonly used term that defines the series of changes that happen to a living creature over the course of its lifetime.

The term "legacy" refers to something that is received from someone who has died.

The "framework" lays down a path to describe the way our relationship with God, self, family and finances progress with time through the general stages of learning, training, rising, consolidating, legacy, and counsel. Bearing in mind that there will likely be overlap across stages, we'll go right into a description of the framework. You'll be able to easily build the story you want your life to be, while looking at the story it has become thus far and how this has progressed with time.

A Framework for Living

Legacy:
Vision:
Values:

TIMELINE	GOD	SELF	FAMILY	FINANCE	AGE	PHASE
1965					0	Learning
1990					25	Learning
2000					35	Training
2010					45	Rising
2014					49	
2015					50	
Q1						
Q2						
Q3						
Q4						Consolidating
2016					51	
2017					52	
2018					53	
2019					54	
2020					55	
2021					56	
2022					57	
2023					58	
2024					59	
2025					60	Legacy
2026					61	
2027					62	
2028					63	
2029					64	
2030					65	
2035					70	Counsel

Goal:

Figure 3.1 A Framework for Adrian's Legacy-Building

35

Can I get an Idea of My Legacy?

We are using the definition of legacy to mean something received from someone who has died. If that is the case, one could argue that you cannot know your legacy for certain because it is only born when you die. Without splitting hairs, I am going to assume that it is possible to project your legacy and then to use it to direct your life's energies. Let's trace the thought.

By now you may have already defined your vision: what you want to be as a person. You may also have defined your values: the way you are prepared to behave in order to become what you want to be. This is how we defined these terms in chapter 2.

On the strength of these two pillars, you may be able to think about this question: "What do I want to be known for after I die?" Think about this more as what you want to be identified with rather than what you want to be famous for, if that helps to release you from any unwanted sense of arrogance.

To reiterate, my life vision is to recognize the image of God in every person I meet. I want to be a part of helping individuals to open up to the potential God has placed in them, and to be a champion for removal of obstacles placed in peoples' lives by others who seek to control them with ulterior and selfish motives.

And I value the fulfillment that comes with knowing that I am "chasing after God" and trying to do what I believe He expects of me in every situation, with the right heart attitude.

To me then, a legacy aspiration is that Africa will rise in my lifetime, and I will be identified with that rise. I am a Canadian who was born and raised in Africa. My children are Canadian, and my life is in Canada. However, particularly in a world that is increasingly globally integrated, spans of influence do not need to be locally bound.

Nelson Mandela aspired to a South Africa that would be free of racial oppression and he risked his life by staying there and fighting for it, paying the price of twenty-seven years in jail, and eventually becoming its first black President. David Livingstone, a nineteenth century medical missionary who had an aspiration for Africa, left his homeland in Scotland in pursuit of it. William Wilberforce, an English politician and Evangelical Christian, had an aspiration for the abolition of the slave trade from Africa, and he remained in his homeland (England) in pursuit of that.

The support tapestry is wide and you don't have to be in Africa in order to positively impact Africa. Can I craft a pathway to my aspiration while serving the Canadian homeland that I love and cherish? I can and I am.

Now, the legacy aspiration is usually very much a dream and often not something tangible. It is useful to include a multi-year goal (two or three years) that is concrete, difficult but achievable, and specific enough in detail that you can measure it and set up an action plan to get it. This goal must be a milestone that is relevant to your legacy aspiration. You describe it in language that suggests that it has already been accomplished: it is a reality.

One example of a piece of this is a mortgage. You may need to take a twenty five year mortgage down to fifteen years in order to free up legacy resources later on. A goal to restructure payments over the next three years would have implications for the other important compartments in your life. We will drill deeper into this in subsequent chapters.

Phases of a Typical Life Cycle

I have described the phases of a typical life cycle in the order of learning, training, rising, consolidating, legacy, and counsel. The time ascribed to each phase is approximate only, and there may be some overlap and out of sequence moments in your experience. As a general model to understand how my life has developed, and comparing notes with others who are further along and even beyond the cycle, what I will describe is a good fit for my own experience and observation. Thus, I will describe each phase in a little more detail.

I saw a hilariously accurate poster that encouraged teenagers who have had enough of being harassed by their parents to do something about it immediately. They should move out and get a job right away, so that they can pay their own way while they still know everything.

I want to clarify upfront that I am very optimistic about teens as a demographic. As I write this, I have two teen children who are my pride and joy and who bring indescribable flavor to my quality of life. I think it is very important, however, for people to recognize that there is a season in life for concentrated learning about how the world functions.

The learning phase of the life cycle is the period when people learn "facts" and "schools of thought" about how things work. Our society is generally structured to accommodate dedicated learning through the ages zero to about twenty five. I don't suggest that learning stops at twenty five, but rather that this period in life is generally accepted as one where people have a focus on absorbing information for base learning.

This basic level of education became apparent to me when I took my first mathematics class at university and found the course title to be "An *Introduction* to Mathematics" after I had already received the top grade in the General Certificate of Education (*Advanced* Level) Mathematics at high school. I would go on to understand that my honors degree in Electrical Engineering gave me basic entry level knowledge to learn how to practice in the field of Engineering.

The concept does not apply to academic learning alone. The same is true of trade apprenticeships, military training and so forth. It extends to every area of life.

The training phase of the life cycle is the time to apply our learning under advisement as a focus in our development. I have loosely framed this period in the twenty five to thirty five year range. This has very little to do with the function, role or level we assume and very much to do with the way we make effective decisions. Input from supervisors, mentors, industry experts and parents are only some examples of the sources of advisement that guide the training phase.

In the Electrical Engineering field there was a structured professional training program with increasing levels of technical and management rigor that led to a professional engineering designation. Recognized engineering professionals, both in the company and in wider industry environments, acted as mentors in this. The same can be found in many other organized areas of life – professional, vocational, personal etc.

The rising phase of the life cycle is the one where people tend to find a few focal points within them that come together, and I identify this period as the thirty five to forty five year bracket. The issue is that life is very busy during this period with external draw from growing children, aging parents, a competitive work environment and personal needs, to name just a few. The conflicting pulls can often lead to a loss of perspective and then to a release in the wrong areas that result in compromise to the longer-term purposes.

The example that spoke significantly to me may be counter-intuitive yet it made sense to me because growth or rising is not usually evident to the "naked eye" so to speak. Here's my example.

In the Far East, there is a tree called the Chinese bamboo tree. This remarkable tree is different from most trees in that it doesn't grow in the usual fashion. While most trees grow steadily over a period of years, the Chinese bamboo tree doesn't break through the ground for the first four years. Then, in the fifth year, an amazing thing happens – the tree begins to grow at an astonishing rate. In fact, in a period of just five weeks, a Chinese bamboo tree can grow to a height of 90 feet. It's almost as if you can actually see the tree growing before your very eyes.

The key to the break through is to keep watering the tree you've planted even when you can't see it rising above ground level, because all the "rising" is actually occurring below ground level. This is what is going to hold the future.

For me this period marked a fast rise in professional, spiritual and community responsibility. And with it came the pressure to "cash in". As an example, I began to down play the significance of my professional responsibility and even though I worked at maximum capacity, in my attitude I began to "throw my pearls before the swine". While I was grateful to God for His provision in this area of professional responsibility, I lost sight of the privilege of what I had, and began to talk about its inability to satisfy me. Well, after going through the inner movements of being restructured out of two companies in as many years, I rediscovered the significance of this focus in my life.

The consolidation phase in the life cycle comes in the forty five to fifty five year period. This is generally the period – it could be sooner or later – where the draws on you begin to shed as children become independent, parents pass on, life experience helps to weather the competitive work environment, and the nature of personal needs start to mature. The freed up bandwidth allows you to lift your head up and begin to see the Chinese bamboo shoots of your life begin to break through the ground and grow upwards rapidly.

The danger here is that people realize that we have not planted well for we don't like the fruit that's coming out of our past. Bill Hybels has built a very effective megachurch in Chicago and has helped leaders globally in their development. He counsels that this is a time to *not* do anything drastic that you might regret, but to stay the course. It's easy to dig up the roots of the bamboo shoot with the intention of planting roots that we prefer, except that we have to factor in the time it took to get to this point and evaluate it against the time we potentially have ahead.

I need to insert a specific insight here. I am not suggesting that it's too late to make changes. The legendary Colonel Sanders started the Kentucky Fried Chicken franchise when he was over sixty years old and moved from being someone dependent on a social security check to one of the richest people in America. So if you're reaping bad fruit in an area of your life that is emotionally charged, getting objective input from someone who you trust and who has a track record in that area is definitely a good idea. That said, I am suggesting that it is *usually* more important to tend the garden you now have rather than tossing it out.

The legacy phase is between years fifty five and sixty five. You have amassed the wisdom, experience and knowledge to be able to understand what is important to you, and how you can use your resources most effectively.

The counsel phase is from sixty five to seventy. I have used seventy as the end point based on Psalm 90: 10: "The days of our lives are seventy years; And if by reason of strength they are eighty years, Yet their boast is only labor and sorrow; For it is soon cut off, and we fly away." So, I plan based on seventy years and will gladly accept God's adjustment either way.

It is amazing to me to listen to the wisdom of the elders. I have frequently marveled at the simplicity of the language and real life examples they use. I heard such a story from an older foreman at a plant I once managed, about three bulls grazing in a farmer's pen. The farmer wanted to grow his herd and placed three cows in the neighboring pen. The youngest bull looked across and said to the other two bulls, "Let's charge down the fence and go for those cows next door." The older bull said to the younger one, "Hold on, there's a gate towards the corner on the adjoining fence and it's open. Let's just go through it." The oldest of the three bulls was busy munching grass when the two younger ones asked if he was coming. The old bull looked across and said, "Leave the gate open and let's keep grazing. They'll come onto our side when they're ready".

The elders' understanding of conduct and timing can save us lots of struggle and reward us with unprecedented access.

Time Line

In the first column of the Excel sheet you can enter incremental years for each year from where you currently are to seventy. Then take the current year and enter four rows, one for each quarter. I have found that one quarter (three months) is enough time to allow you to achieve a step change towards your annual goal, but not too long to risk loss of focus on the activity necessary to take the step.

Now with an end game and broad road map in view, you can put down milestones that are of interest to you along the journey to seventy. Some people call this a bucket list. It should contain purpose checkpoints as well as rewards. For example, receiving an Engineering Degree in 2018 could be one item, while another is visiting Fairmont Banff Springs in 2019. Determine these check points in an atmosphere of prayer and pay attention to thoughts that intrigue you. Remember that this will be a dynamic list that will develop over the years but I think that the core won't change very much with time.

My formal education was framed using this format. I planned to get an Engineering degree to learn how to *create* physical wealth. I worked in mining and was involved in extracting high value metals from essentially worthless dirt in the ground. Then I obtained a Business degree with the goal of learning how to *control* wealth. Finally, I took a Divinity degree to *comprehend* it; in other words, to understand the purpose of all this: to answer the "why". And I had targets for achieving these along my time line. It happened as I had planned it, against the odds.

Compartment Interplay

The milestones we lay out are along the lines of the four categories: God, self, family and finances. In subsequent chapters I will go into each of these categories in some detail. At this point it is important to show that there is interplay between the categories. I'll try to illustrate this by way of an example.

When I was studying to get my Masters degree in Business, my key area of focus was finances. This is in the sense that I was in the learning phase of my life and this particular education and qualification would be an instrumental building block in my ability to achieve my life financial goals. My God goal was low on formal ministry and high on cultural exposure by attending a black British church. My self-goal was quite modest – eat to live. My family goal was to use discretionary time to get to know my new wife.

When I began my Masters degree in Divinity ten years later, I was in the rising phase of my life. With family assuming a much more significant place in the balance and God requiring a much more hands on ministry involvement, and the education attached to this "God" category rather than finances, the emphases were very different.

Conclusion

This then is the framework I have used to bring some sense to my journey. Let me conclude with an immigrant's experience of entry into the Canadian labor market. When I applied for roles similar to the one I left in Zimbabwe, employers told me that I had no Canadian experience. When I applied for roles closer to entry level, they told me I was over-qualified. Eventually a temp agency manager had pity on me, literally, and took me on. As I did basic contract assignments such as garbage compacting in warehouses, I "knew" (so I thought) that God had me on a trajectory to meaningful contribution. I read my goals and plans sheet everyday, actually believed what I was reading, and acted as though everything was right on track. In the third month I received the "temp of the month award". It was deathly tough on many fronts but I knew that I didn't have the luxury of looking at that. I still don't have that luxury. The framework has worked and is working for me.

How about you? I think if you simply take the Excel spreadsheet (Figure 3.1) and plot the things you want to achieve when you want to achieve them, that would be a powerful visual start to your pathway. Perhaps you now have some vision and value thoughts that you can also insert. If you do this, you'll begin to get the sense, "I am going somewhere".

And if you've done this type of exercise in another form in the past, do it again now as a refresher. It can only reinforce your aspirations.

CHAPTER 4

WHAT DOES GOD WANT FROM ME?

He hath shown thee, O man, what is good: and what
doth the Lord require of thee but to do justly and to
love mercy, and to walk humbly with thy God?
- Micah 6: 8

For You do not desire sacrifice, or else I would
give it. You do not delight in burnt offering.
The sacrifices of God are a broken spirit,
A broken and a contrite heart – These,
O God, You will not despise.
- Psalm 51: 16 – 17

Introduction

God is my anchor. He occupies the first and most important pillar
or compartment of my life. Quite apart from the benefits I believe
I will have with Him after I die, I experience tremendous benefits
during my daily life as a result of my faith in God. It is faith
in God that has kept me optimistic and enjoying myself when
circumstances might have suggested otherwise. For example,
when I was looking for my first job after arriving in Canada, I

was convinced that God had purpose for me in each meeting I had. Therefore, even interviews that did not result in job offers were valuable to me. For me, it took the force of faith in God to maintain this perspective.

Being satisfied in my own mind, then, that there is no one or nothing else more capable than God is to keep me steady, I need to know what He requires from me so that I may get the highest benefit from attaching myself to Him.

What is most important to God? I certainly believe that for human beings, getting into a right relationship with Him is what He wants most. And I have also come to understand that there are innumerable things in the Bible that are evidently important to God. In the context of this writing, therefore, I find it more relevant to pose the question from my personal vantage point. What are the things that stand out to *me* that are important to God? To me there are two main things: my heart attitude and my predisposition towards other people.

Please remember that this isn't necessarily *your* anchor, and these aren't necessarily your main things. Only be satisfied that *your* anchor is most capable of keeping you steady, and that you have identified the things that are most important to your anchor. From here on in this chapter I shall tell the story of what God finds most important where I am concerned. You will have the chance to think about what points of attachment you must identify, and begin to lay them down.

I wrote earlier that God is very interested in a heart that has right intentions. In my experience, *authenticity* is very important to this end. We must learn what is right, accept it and then determine to live outwardly what we have chosen to believe inwardly. To the extent that there is a gap here, we might feel the tension of dissonance within that will trouble us inwardly.

I believe that Martin Luther may have felt this very thing at the dawn of the Reformation that birthed Protestant Christians out from the Catholic church in Europe in the sixteenth century. When being pressured to recant and withdraw the positions he had publicly taken against specific Catholic church teachings, he said that his conscience would not allow him to withdraw his criticisms. Unless the Bible showed that he was wrong, Luther would remain resolute in his stand. He maintained this even in the face of death.

It would be an over simplification to imagine that this was easy and that Luther was some type of super hero. He did not begin this particular campaign of discourse with a mind to leave the Catholic church. When he was eventually required to officially respond to the direction to recant he took a day to think it through, even though he had defended his position many times before. The next day his first response was long-winded and not definitive. When pressed, his second response was, "My conscience is a prisoner of God's Word. I cannot and will not recant, for to disobey one's conscience is neither just nor safe. God help me. Amen."[9]

In addition to authenticity's contribution to having a heart with right intentions, there is *communication*. I believe that we can train ourselves to line our communication up with who we are inside: to find our own voice *literally* if you will. Learning the skills to communicate authentically positions our hearts to be effectively used for things that God is concerned about.

Now, people and circumstances will always have an opinion about who and what you are, and they will make you into what you know you are not if you allow them to. If you've ever told someone about something you dream of accomplishing, and they've said to you (in word or attitude), "Who do you think you are?" you understand what I mean. People, sometimes even close to you, can be offended by your ambition for no logical reason.

You can't please everyone. Like the ugly duckling,[10] you need to find your *swans* because they will recognize you and God will use you. But don't *cast your pearls before swine.* If you know you have something of value to offer people, and your particular audience is rejecting what you have, it may be better to stop offering it to them. They will disrespect you and God's gifting in you. Is this too strong? I apologize: please try to look beyond any offence to see the point.

The incredible thing is that God is also very interested in other people. Specifically, He is active in vessels of *justice and mercy.* Attributes of wisdom, organizational and logistical intelligence, and empathy can all be developed. And these skills can be used to channel justice and mercy to others.

People tell me that I communicate well in both verbal and written forms. Those who are close to me say that I am genuine in my communication, and that I communicate what I think is right in the way that I think is right. I have also been described as intelligent and empathetic. Am I bragging? No. Rather, I think about it this way: environments that require these attributes of me put me in the best position to do what pleases God. I am much less likely to do that using other attributes that I am much less recognized for and not at ease with. And I don't thrive in environments that don't need what I've got.

Weaving these concepts into my story may make them clearer.

What is it about the Human Heart that gets God's Attention?

It was the Prophet Jeremiah who said that the heart is deceitful above all things, and desperately wicked; who can know it? (Jeremiah 17: 9) And it was King David who penned the thought that God would not despise a broken and a contrite heart. (Psalm 51: 17) He wrote this after stealing his loyal soldier's wife, trying to cover it up, plotting and achieving his assassination through the enemy's sword, and then passing hypocritical judgment upon someone who he thought did the same thing in principle. Don't miss the fact that David only felt this way after he had been found out.

David was the ancient Israelite king who led the final conquest of all the land God had promised the nation. During one campaign, David remained in the capital, Jerusalem, while his army went to battle. While on his palace roof he saw a woman bathing and discovered that she was the wife of one of his most loyal soldiers. David's desire had the better of him and he took the woman and committed adultery with her. When she became pregnant he called for her husband to return from the battle in the hope that he would sleep with his wife and somehow cover the offence. But the soldier would not touch his wife out of solidarity with his comrades who were in the field. David then sent the soldier back with a letter for the army general. He was to have the soldier spearhead an attack and then withdraw support from him. In this way, the enemy was able to kill the soldier. David then took his widow as his own wife.

One of the roles the king occupied was that of a judge in Israel. One day a prophet came before him and explained the case of a rich man with many herds. He had a guest come to visit him. In order to feed his guest, he went to a poor neighbor who only had one lamb and forcibly took that lamb and slaughtered it. David was angry when he heard of this injustice and his sentence was not only for the man to repay the lamb fourfold, but also that he was to die. The prophet then said to him, "You are that man". It was only then that David expressed sorrow for what he had done.

There are two things about our hearts that get God's attention: their depravity and their repentance or genuine regret for wrongdoing. Over time I have developed a very strong sense of right and wrong. I've noticed that it seems to require much discipline to remain inclined towards what is right, and no discipline to lean towards what is wrong. This is indeed debatable, for it takes tremendous resilience to live with the consequences of choosing what is wrong. But I digress: it still *seems* to require much discipline to lean to what is right. Depravity then, from the dawn of my memory to the streams echoing in my soul as I write this, is an ever-present option.

And yet, the consciousness that I have turned from this and looked towards God synonymously draws His Being all through me, displacing the reach that depravity has for me. Access is one way: I would have to reach past God's presence, so to speak, to find depravity for it cannot reach in to find me. God knows when we're desperate in our sin, in going against His will for us, and He knows when we turn towards Him.

By definition, the intentions of a depraved heart are not authentic. Its host tends to act with ulterior motives and therefore experiences the strain of pretense. When the inner and the outer person are pulling in different directions, it can tear the heart.

When I was eighteen and at university, I finally took a stand and chose to live for God. This followed a struggle of several years to find the right level of compromise and I finally sold out to a full pursuit of God's desire for me. This meant giving up some things and places that had time and again taken me into areas that I knew were not pleasing to God. For the first time that I could remember, I felt complete inner peace and the absence of tension, that conflict between right and wrong.

Barry (alias) was a law student. He was relentless in his opposition to the stand I had taken and challenged me about the pitfalls of my decision every time he saw me. He extolled the *virtues* of wine, women and song and frequently volunteered to make any and all of these available to me at his expense. I kept making my case and declining his offers.

It was a Friday evening on campus and I had just returned to my room after yet another prayer meeting where I had failed to receive the gift of speaking in tongues as I had read in the Bible. This gift is one where the recipient prays using language not learned in advance. It was going on one year now and I was feeling that maybe God didn't care that much about me. My friend Tony (alias) knocked on the door and then jumped onto the bed with a bottle of beer in his hand. At the time he was an atheist and genuinely was – and still is – my good friend. (It's incredible to me how some of my closest friends in life have been either atheists or non-practicing believers.) Tony helped me with a beer and later with a ride to the club. I was feeling really depressed and stood in a corner sipping on another beer.

Then Barry arrived making *a hoopla* of noise and it seemed like he did not know whether he was drunk or sick. When he saw me he called out loudly and came over to me. I was shocked to hear what he had to say. Barry told me how disappointed he was because he thought that in me he had found a genuine man of faith, only to now see me occupied with worthlessness. It turned out that he saw no value in much of the entertainment he had been encouraging me to participate in. Rather, he valued my concern for people, my choice to engage in *clean* fun, and my determination to make a positive difference in society through my life based on the principles of the Bible.

I experienced a lesson that day (experienced, not learned): truth is in you. Don't be fooled by the outer expressions, for that is what human beings look at. But God sees what's inside a person. And he knew what Barry was yearning for.

Heart Skills God can use: Authenticity and Communication

When I asked one of my brothers, as a young teen, what made him so popular with girls he said to me, "You've got to be yourself". For a long time I thought that being myself was about acting out or expressing what my inner man was saying. But if the heart is deceitful, that can be very dangerous. I came to understand that authenticity is not based on your heart telling you what's right, but rather on you telling your heart what's right. Jesus said that it is out of the abundance of the heart that the mouth speaks. (Matthew 12: 34) The idea here is that people will eventually say or do what they believe, or what is predominantly on their mind. When I see my daughter Andrea's attitude and words change after she's been with her friends, I am reminded that "abundance" can be received from the environment. So authenticity is not only about being who you are, but also about becoming who you want to be. Let me share an example.

I think that my wife is the most beautiful woman in the world. When I say this, some people argue with me mentally and sometimes even verbally. But that means that they miss the point. I don't make that statement for them I make it for myself. Before I asked Lucy to marry me, someone told me that a man ought not to propose to a woman unless he is certain that she is the best woman alive. Somehow that made deep sense to me intuitively. I wasn't sure that Lucy was the best if only because I hadn't met all the women alive. But in order to enjoy the satisfaction of a secure, biblical marriage, I would need to be sure. So I made the choice, and decided from that point until now that she is the best. At first this didn't seem logical but at some point it became truth. Suddenly she was my only possible, most beautiful bible fulfilling wife. Thus, my heart became what I wanted it to be, and it is in harmony with my expression towards my wife.

Constant application of God's truth to your heart can cause you to become that truth: authentically.

Now in communication, I have learned that real heart connections are made when we genuinely believe what we are communicating. Sales training often teaches that salespeople must know their product intimately and believe that it meets clients' needs in a superior manner if they are to be top performers.

In addition to belief, it is very important to understand that there are nuances to the way different cultures communicate. Therefore, it is important to learn what *mechanisms* are effective: clothing, tone of voice, choice of language, facial expression and so forth.

The third pillar is credibility in communication. When you build up a reputation that you can be trusted to do the right thing, there is a lower probability that people second-guess your message.

Communication belief, style and credibility are skills that can be learned with time and focus. God is relational, and communication is a central part of relationship. So since God is important to me, I have also put lots of time into developing communication.

What do I have to do with Other People?

Justice and mercy are very important to God. Justice is about righteousness and being fair according to a right standard. Mercy is about forgiving someone the punishment they deserve when it is in your power and right to administer it. Determining justice and mercy in the human context is difficult since we are all creatures of our own will and perspective, and we really cannot know what is inside another person's heart. The Mosaic law laid down parameters to facilitate administration of justice and mercy but, even then, people were unable to get it right. This is one of the reasons that Christians rely so heavily on the presence of God's spirit in our lives, to help us to make the right assessments.

Given its complexity, understanding the norms of a particular society and their application in a generally acceptable manner is a skill to be developed. Not only is this used for self-governance, but also in relation to decisions affecting others. Those who are able to demonstrate visible levels of proficiency in this domain are said to have wisdom.

The ability to create some level of order out of chaos is another important skill. This requires logic and organization. It enables people to work effectively together and we achieve more together than we do alone. But in order to achieve this, we cannot be using our energy to nullify the efforts of the next person. Effective organization draws on logistical skills that set us up to pull in the same direction.

The third skill in this package is empathy. This is the ability to understand and share the feelings of another. As we learn to put ourselves in the other person's position, we are better able to obey the golden rule: do unto others as you would have them do to you. Wisdom and logic can be cold and inanimate, but empathy is the life that connects the heart to other people.

So, what does God Want from Me?

Let me attempt to bring the ideas together in a brief paragraph: God wants to work through my heart to bring others to an understanding that they can be pardoned for their human failings (mercy), and have equal access (justice) to what He promises. Developing my ability to organize and inspire people opens them up to me so that I can share with them the great truths that have given me liberty in this life, and they can take it even further in their own lives.

This has led to some milestones in my walk with God.

1. Being born again was to have a right heart.
2. Going to seminary was to learn in depth God's recorded wisdom.

3. Seeking pastoral leadership was to learn personal Godly influence with a variety of people.
4. Preaching was to communicate authentically to peoples' hearts.
5. Engaging in international ministry was to organize access through complex environments with deliberate impact.

So now I'll wrap it up by returning to my life goals:

I want to use my organizational training and understanding of God's truth to encourage the best in people at home so that they will be willing to partner with me in imparting what we have to less fortunate but equally deserving people both at home and abroad.

Spiritually and in our sphere of influence, we'll feed Canada to feed the world. And somewhere in all this, Africa will rise in my lifetime. Africa has been blessed with her share of natural wealth, much of which supports elevated standards of living in other parts of the world. Yet many people in Africa do not enjoy the benefits of that wealth. This is not necessary and, more importantly to me, is not what God wants, in my opinion. We have the capacity to partner with our brothers and sisters in Africa and share ways to raise their level of self-sufficiency.

Conclusion

What is it in your life that you have entrusted to keep your mind stable in the face of any turmoil that may come around? Can your anchor deliver on your expectation? What does your anchor require of you in order to deliver for you? Take the time to reflect on this. Translate your reflection into milestones that you can place on your time line under your first column heading. Be patient with yourself as you go through this. Be expectant in your pursuit as you gain ground.

CHAPTER 5

SELFLESS OR SELFISH?

You hypocrite, first take the plank out of your
own eye, and then you will see clearly to remove
the speck from your brother's eye.
- Matthew 7: 5 (NIV)

For if a man cannot manage his own household,
how can he take care of God's church?
- 1 Timothy 3: 5 (NLT)

Introduction

Chapter 5 "Selfless or Selfish?" is about taking care of yourself
so that you can make the entire journey of life before you as
effectively as possible. An example may crystallize this idea for
some of us.

Your car at a very basic level is a means of transforming energy
stored in fuel into motion. You go along for the ride with little to
no exertion of your own energy at a rate that far exceeds what you
could achieve directly using your own strength. If you take care
of the car, it takes care of your transportation wishes. Taking care
of your car involves things like maintaining it, refreshing its oil,

not letting it stand idle for long periods of time in bad weather, and not over-exerting it beyond what it is designed for.

Your body and your emotions may be likened to a car. If you maintain them well and exercise them wisely in deliberate environments, you equip them well to carry you through life's journey. Equally important is the capacity this creates to enable others to come along with you for the ride. I understand that accidents do happen, but that possibility doesn't justify reckless driving, both of your car and of your person. We do what is in our control for our upkeep, and leave what is outside of our control to God.

So my key question in this chapter is about trade off: where is the pivot line between being selfless versus being selfish?

Wayne Cordeiro wrote a book called, "Leading on Empty: Refilling Your Tank and Renewing Your Passion". He describes his experience of being burnt out and his recovery from it. Wayne pastors a megachurch in Hawaii and his outer success may seem out of step with his inner deficit. But isn't that so often the case, even with people who seem to be doing a tremendous amount of good externally? Which is why taking care of myself is the second most important pillar of my framework.

To be selfish is to be concerned chiefly with one's own profit or pleasure. To be selfless is to be concerned more with the needs and wishes of others than with one's own. I would like to make the case that taking care of yourself first can be a very selfless act when your aspirations are to serve the greater good. However, I think it is more difficult to define boundary lines in living this out. My advice is best articulated in the classic Greek aphorism: *Know thyself.*

In our temporal world we are able to accomplish things by using our energy, either mental or physical. While vision, goal setting and the like are used to focus our energy so we can use it most productively (the most output for the least input), we must first generate the energy before we can use it. I would like to discuss three things that generate mental energy, and three things that generate physical energy. Rest, stimulation and psychological conditions are inputs that cause our mental energy to come alive. Food, exercise and bodily applications are determinants of our physical energy level.

When more energy is required of us than we are generating, our tank drains and when it's empty we burn out. So we need to prioritize what things are drawing our energy and either eliminate the excess or supplement what fills us. Most of us have enough energy to take care of the basic things God requires of us as human beings. You may not have enough energy to take care of a church but you do have enough to take care of your family. However, if the church comes before the family and your energy is short, you may end up failing your church and then your family as well. Hence, the apostle Paul advises Timothy that a man must first know how to rule his own house before he can take care of the church of God. (1 Timothy 3: 5) *Walk* with me through some thoughts.

How can I get Mental Energy for Good Insight and Decisions?

The Bible tells us that God created the heavens and the earth in six days, and He then rested on the seventh day. (Genesis 2: 2) The Mosaic law used this precedent to separate the seventh (Sabbath) day for the people to rest. (Exodus 20: 8 – 11) Also, the people were not to cultivate the land in the seventh year so it could rest. (Leviticus 25) In a very practical way, Jesus took His disciples away to a lonely place where they could rest after they had been teaching and caring for the people. (Mark 6: 31) *Rest* is an important restorative process.

Rest can occur in at least two forms: sleep, and relaxation from stressful activity.

Although science does not have a single definitive answer for why we sleep, understanding some of the theories that have developed can motivate us to respect sleep's functions more and enjoy the health benefits it affords. After all, we sleep for about one third of our lives.

It is believed that sleep has both a cognitive and physiological role. Well-rested people tend to be able to learn new concepts more readily than tired people. Also, people who have a good sleep after learning new concepts tend to have higher retention levels than those who don't have a good sleep. This is why we are often advised to "sleep on it" before making a major decision.

Experiments have shown that animals deprived entirely of sleep lose all immune function and die in just a matter of weeks. Also, studies have shown that many of the major restorative functions in the body like muscle growth, tissue repair, protein synthesis, and growth hormone release occur mostly, or in some cases only, during sleep.

Add to this the fact that babies are irritable when they are tired (as are adults), and this supports the case for being intentional about the amount of sleep we get. [11]

Rest doesn't only come from sleep. Recreation is also very important, and this is something I am not very good at. I always feel a sense of urgency to be productive. This is why I don't enjoy driving, especially long-distance, for I can use that time much more productively reading or taking a power nap. But I do recognize the vitality of relaxation and I do set aside time for that, especially with my family.

Stimulation is a second factor that makes our mental energy come alive. Things that raise our interest or curiosity tend to raise our level of alertness. I've seen it so many times: people falling asleep during a meeting become lively in conversation as soon as the meeting ends.

My Mum had a second hand store when I was in secondary school. I was in the store one time when a customer came in and began to talk to her about his teenage son. He said that he overheard his son singing a song by Bob Marley. Not only did the son have all the words, but he also had all the inflections, accent and timing mimicked perfectly. The man marveled at how his son could learn the song so exactly, but he couldn't learn history at school to pass his exams.

I'm telling this story over thirty years later because it was profound to me. People tend to do what they want to do. This is why I decided to pay attention to understanding what excites me. Then I learned that I have to be intentional about periodically going to where those things are either mentally or physically in order to revive my enthusiasm. I can subsequently return to the routine work that is necessary for success and tackle it with the newly acquired energy.

I have also learned the importance of *riding the wave.* The image I have here is of a surfer being carried on the crest of a tall wave several times his/her height. When you are on a high, take all the territory you can. When you hit low points, learn to conserve energy.

Psychological conditions tie into this piece, and this is the third factor that I've found important in topping up my mental energy. I believe that frames of mind, or "thinking moods", can be created. And I think that frames of mind restrict, maintain or regenerate mental capacity. My observation is also that different frames of mind suit people differently, perhaps as a function of their personality. Maybe an example will highlight this better.

I don't like interpersonal conflict because my experience is that it is counter productive. I need to make myself understood on this point. Mental sparring in order to get to the best outcome is not what I am talking about here: pursuit of excellence through exchange and challenge of ideas is critically important. It's the battles of the ego that frustrate me. These are the ones where we argue in order to not lose face, and not necessarily out of conviction that what we are presenting is the best option. In a word, it's more about "pride" than anything else. I feel that this is a waste of time and resources.

I have enjoyed a rich range of cultural exposure. Fully aware of the danger of stereotyping, I nonetheless feel that the case I will describe may best make my point clear. As I grew up, I noticed that the status associated with evangelical clergy was very important to them. To me, it defeated the purpose of the function, namely servant leadership. To this day my mind disengages when I am in the presence of people who project an expectation of importance because of that position. While I know that God expects us to respect the position, I don't think he expects the position to *demand* that respect.

I was in a meeting where we were working on setting up strategies for church leadership. We had broken up into small groups for discussion. It became clear after a few minutes that our group leader had limited understanding of strategy. However, he pastored a church and pushed that lever early on. I am not saying that this is right, but I will tell you what happened to me. I checked out.

I have been in church strategy meetings facilitated by someone who travelled the world helping successful companies to revise their strategies. Our little group didn't intimidate him, he didn't need to demand respect for he was confident with his trade, and that set the tone that got me engaged and pulled ideas out of me.

Strategies for topping up your mental energy could change with time. As a twenty five year old, eight hours sleep might be ideal (though rare) and driving by the big houses might light your candle. As a fifty year old, six hours sleep may be all you can take and hearing from an underprivileged child you support tops up your energy. The key is to listen to your heart and to know yourself.

What Contributes to my Physical Energy Level?

I was a slim and very athletic teen during my youth. One of the goals foremost in my mind for a long time was to gain weight. I went on various fattening diets and had the best time ever with food going through my early twenties without gaining weight. Then I got married…

I've heard many people talk about the way that body change has crept up on them. People who have been athletic in their youth carry the mindset that they are still athletic into their thirties without the same level of bodily activity and metabolic rate. Then they decide to participate in a game or event and find that "the spirit is willing but the flesh is weak". What they thought they were able to do based on prior experience evades them as their bodies simply fail to do what they once were able to do. For me, I had my calves tighten in spasms during the second half of a soccer game. Others have broken bones, pulled muscles that take significantly longer to heal, and so forth. I'll tell my story concerning physical energy to illustrate some of the things I've learned.

I was running a large factory and there were a number of managers there who were bigger than I was – at least that's what I thought. One day I was inspecting a section with one of the managers. As he led me to a particular area, he walked over a freight scale and I quickly glanced at the screen. As I walked over the scale I continued to watch the screen and to my amazement the digits edged higher than his. It gradually settled in my mind over the space of a few seconds that I was actually bigger than the man I had thought was big. More importantly, I realized that I probably looked quite different from the dated mental picture I had of myself. I knew then that I needed to do something to change my physical condition because I was *too young to be that old.*

As part of the benefit package for a number of years, I had access to an annual three hour full medical examination. Each year I saw some of the key metrics tracking in the wrong direction. Being a results oriented individual, I decided to change the nature of conversation I kept having with the physician. So, I changed some things.

I decided to eat according to the Canadian Food Guide. I should mention that I have never liked fruit and I found vegetables unpalatable. Red meat had been a staple for me from close to birth living in the region where some of the world's best beef was reared. My change in diet turned four decades of eating habits on its head. I lost over thirty pounds in three months and remained within three pounds of my ideal weight for the next five years. I had had stiffness in my lower back that I thought was the result of a car accident almost twenty years ago. Remarkably, that stiffness eased away as my weight dropped.

My learning is this: know yourself and what you eat. After doing research on what we should and should not eat, I jokingly came to the conclusion that if I did not eat anything I would have the best chance for a long life. The only problem is that I would starve to death first. So I've learned to pay attention to what my body responds well to and what causes me discomfort. As an example, over the past few years I have significantly reduced my starch intake. I feel much more nimble and energetic at my current weight and diet than I can recall from my mid twenties to early forties.

The physician at my annual medicals gave me an excellent phrase: weight is controlled at the table, and wellness in the gym. So, once my weight was under control, I turned my attention to my wellness. As it turned out, my family was at a stage where we needed a team activity that would offer both discipline and recreation. So we found a karate dojo and determined to go together as a family to the level of black belt. The Sensei (teacher) smiled when we told him our goal and suggested that we take it one step at a time. I was committed to go all the way, even though I couldn't imagine myself as a black belt. The exercises were usually basic and once we got into the routine, karate became something like a pulse in my life. The self-control necessary to hold certain postures, and to keep emotions in check during sparring sessions, proved to be an incredible reinforcement for the discipline and life skills required for success everyday. Again, my physical energy level turned up and I was able to handle a very hectic schedule with much more ease. It was only after I stopped karate training around six years later that it became very evident what good shape my body was in.

The Bible says that bodily exercise profits little, but spiritual exercise profits much. (1Timothy 4: 8) I misunderstood this principle for a long time. For certain, the spiritual disciplines are number one. It is of prime concern that we have our spirits in the right place, and that we maintain habits that will *keep* our spirits in that place. This will bring us many benefits.

My misinterpretation was to have no bodily exercise and to think that my spirituality would cover for it. That's bad stewardship. If my body runs out before God's spiritual mandate for my life runs out, I may not be as effective as I could be. The scripture verse does not say that bodily exercise profits *nothing,* but that it profits *little*. I know that in business we take all the profit we can get, because profit is the *gain* we have over the input cost. By analogy, therefore, I wanted to also benefit from the little gain that physical exercise brings.

Once again, I think it is important to know yourself, and to recognize where you are in your life cycle. I've stopped doing karate because the demands on my life pillars have shifted as the things I need to accomplish have progressed. What is important is that I have an adequate level of physical activity to support the energy level I need in order to achieve what God has called me to achieve.

I have a short note on bodily applications. I only want to point here to the importance of using your body in the right way. I have a corporate job and spend several hours during the day behind a computer. There was a time when I experienced a different type of pain than I had known before in my lower back. I think that this may have been because I was not sitting with the right ergonomic posture. So I changed this after having a number of checks with the doctor and things have returned to normal now. I will no longer play competitive soccer, look directly at the sun with my naked eyes or lift heavy weight items using my back rather than my legs. These and similar actions could put me down and restrict my mobility and hence ability to achieve things that are mine to achieve.

Conclusion

In summary then, I am deliberate about what I need to do in order to maximize my mental and physical energy. Without this, I won't have the stamina to do the things that will feed my life's aspirations. And while the relative emphasis may change with time, to use Wayne Cordeiro's analogy, I need to focus on what fills up or drains my tank at any given time period, and move the balance to what prevents me from becoming drained.

Here is the essence of this chapter. First apply the time and resource you have to fulfill what you need – to be distinguished from what you want – before you can help others. This isn't selfish if you end up using most of what you have to then help others.

Learn what you need to keep you going – it usually isn't a large portion of what you have. But don't feel guilty about serving yourself the essentials first. This will set you up to be selfless without breaking yourself in the process. But know yourself, and you'll know the pivot line.

If you haven't yet figured this out personally, use my parameters to start to think about it:

- How many hours of sleep do you need before you wake up naturally? Test it over three successive nights and use the duration you're asleep during the third night, pick the time you need to wake up, then count back to the time you need to go to sleep at night.
- What gets your mind going and stimulates agile thinking in you? What external probing really raises your level of mental alertness? Write some of these down and make time to engage them.
- What psychological conditions drain you? Are there any that you flow in? You need to know what these are so you can moderate your engagement to release or preserve your mental energy as necessary.
- How do you feel after you've eaten? For the most part you should feel energized and not weighed down. How closely does your diet match the Canadian Food Guide?
- Can your body take exertion? How much stamina do you have to outrun a criminal? You can build the amount of exercise you feel you need into your daily routine by being deliberate about simple things like taking the stairs instead of the elevator.
- Do you know how to use your body properly? Find out about the right way to lift, sit etc. and match the level of exertion to the way your body is responding.

If you will build up routines around these areas over the next year, doing just enough to increase your energy levels, you will tune up *the machine* to take you where God's Spirit is leading you with the least amount of wasted effort.

Now, you may be wondering, "But where do I get the time for all this?" Hold the thought for now. In the epilogue, after we've covered the last two pillars, I will have a word about balance and scheduling.

CHAPTER 6

WHAT DO I OWE MY FAMILY?

For this cause a man shall leave his father and his mother, and
shall cleave to his wife, and they shall become one flesh.
- Genesis 2: 24 (NASB)

Honor your father and mother, that your days may be
prolonged in the land which the Lord your God gives you.
- Exodus 20: 12 (NASB)

Introduction

Chapter 6 "What do I Owe my Family?" takes us to the third
pillar of our framework. But who is my family? In a sense, family
actually evolves with time and I will share both my experience
and a biblical view on how and why this happens.

One of the significant social issues we face in western
societies today is the changing definition of family. A sub-issue
that flows from this is the tension between the idea of individual
freedom and accountability. Most people I have discussed these
issues with have agreed that people are interdependent. The
disagreement is usually around what level of interdependency
there should be.

This is why the evolving nature of family with time was an important concept for me to grasp. It has helped me to develop a healthy expectation of child rearing and of the limits to my responsibilities. Many people struggle with this and frequently suffer either guilt or apathy. My goal in this chapter is to provide a background against which people can figure out the debt you owe to your family. This refers to the things you are accountable for by virtue of having a family. Then, it's up to each of us to pay our debt.

Diana Ross, a popular American singer, sings the following line in one of her songs: "Do you get what you're hoping for? When you look behind you there's no open door."[12] Condemnation is never helpful in my opinion. You can't relive what you deem to be a failed child rearing, but you can be the right kind of parent going forward.

What is God's Purpose for Family?

My experience in my family has been fabulous. As I look back at my years growing up, I recognize how the intuitive sense of belonging and affirmation built within me a certain security. As I share life with the family I am now privileged to lead, I cannot find words adequate enough to express the depth of purpose and fulfillment I am experiencing. For me, then, family holds a central place.

Before I get to the biblical model for family, I think it is important to speak to the exceptions to the model. If you were never married, are divorced, never had children, are adopted, or live in a community setting: relationship with God is the primary relationship, and He can – and does – create phenomenal relationships in this life outside of the biblical model. However, to write off the biblical model as non-essential would be to deny

God's foundational design and to expose our individual and social minds to serious risk. Therefore, I believe that a serious understanding of God's design for family is a critical component of our ability to keep our minds.

God created man for an exclusive level of intimacy not found with trees, animals or other elements in His creation. This was a unique kind of relationship.

Yet God saw the need to create a second level of intimacy within humanity, second to intimacy with God, but above the level of intimacy we have with the earth, the trees and the animals. So He created a woman uniquely coming out of the man's body, and she fit the design of a helper suitable for him. This is why, when a man gets married, he must replace his primary earthly relationship with his parents, with his marriage relationship as the primary one. He "leaves" his parents and in this sense is "no longer with them". He "cleaves" to his wife and in this sense becomes "one flesh" with her. The word "cleave" describes a connection that is forged to be intimately close. Inasmuch as his flesh came from his parents, the marital intimacy joins his flesh to that of his wife. So we see a movement out of one family and into another one.

The design of this process was to populate the earth and to propagate generations through time. So the man and woman generate children who proceed from their flesh in some ways akin to how the first woman proceeded from the first man's body. The parallel I want to draw here is that the children become part of the family just as the first family came to be – through the extraction and development of flesh. It is a temporal thing – one that belongs to time and not eternity.

In due time the children will find spouses and in order to duplicate the family, they will separate from their birth families. This does not preclude relationships outside the new family, but it does make the new family relationships the primary ones.

The purpose of the family is to provide an intimate place of companionship and fellowship where principles for right living can be passed on and nurtured most effectively. It is from these tight bases that communities can form and grow, with a good balance of structure and vitality that permits societies to successfully develop the earth's resources as God intended. It is the unity created around individual, family and community that propel us forward to subdue the earth.

Family relationships are bound by time, but our individual relationships with God are from conception to eternity. Thus, our familial relationships change from eternity, through the time continuum, and out to eternity. We will use this thought in answering the question, "Who is my family?"

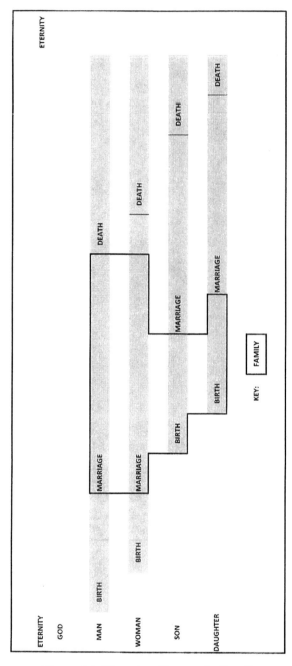

Figure 6.1 Changing Phases of a Family

Who is My Family?

From the time a person is conceived and forever going forward, that person will relate to God. The relationship in eternity will either be one of fellowship, or one of separation. Using different terms, we will either know God personally, or know about Him without experiencing any personal contact with Him. Given that this is the longest relationship and most important, it is the primary one and must be guarded at all costs. If any other relationship must be dissolved in order to maintain this relationship, dissolving it is the best decision.

Quoting Jesus, Luke 14: 26 says, "If you want to be my disciple, you must hate everyone else by comparison – your father and mother, wife and children, brothers and sisters – yes, even your own life. Otherwise, you cannot be my disciple." (NLT) I am using this extreme statement not to undervalue other relationships, but rather to emphasize the relative importance of our relationship with God. To be clear, the word "hate" is not intended to imply that we should wish ill on anybody. Rather, it is a comparative term. Its emphasis is on the absolute priority of a relationship with God.

When we are born into the world, based on the biblical model, our primary relationships are with our earthly family. Our parents, in particular, create the environment to nurture our growth before we even have the knowledge of what we need or the capability to ask for or provide it. Siblings help to create a microcosm of the competitive nature of the wider world without the same inherent dangers because the bond of blood has intuitive meaning. The family is a "safe environment" to learn how to balance the need to take care of self with the value of taking care of the needs of others. At this stage then, my family consists of my parents and siblings.

I think it is important here to insert a reminder that this description is after the biblical model. It is not intended to ignore the experiences of many people who come from families with different structures and dynamics. From my heart I acknowledge and affirm that your experiences are real. Rather, this biblical model is a basic reference frame against which to understand our personal experiences, and hopefully one that can guide our aspirations for our own families going forward.

When a sibling leaves the home to get married, their primary relationship moves from "our" family to the "new" family they have formed with their spouse. In many cases we fail to understand this fundamental design and it leads to difficulties when we don't adjust to the new reality. This new reality crystalized for me from an unlikely source.

My father-in-law was not a practicing Christian. But he was a believer and a very wise man, and he had an uncommon grasp of some biblical principles that he presented as life principles in very common language. Some time after our wedding, we spent our first night at his home. Dad sat with me for a long time into the evening, just chatting. Before we retired for the night he gave me this advice that now I was a married man, it was up to me to build my own home with my wife. We were to raise our own children and enjoy the process. He told me that someone else could not come and tell me what to do because it was my home for me to enjoy. Dad was expressing confidence in my ability to establish and lead my new home and family.

Looking back I surely did not fully understand the implications of what he was saying. But what did dawn on me was the application of leaving and cleaving. To that point I had felt that I needed his permission / affirmation for major decisions that would affect his daughter, or at least I paid close attention to what his opinion might be. Now, his task was over and it rested fully with me. Of course he continued to care deeply for Lucy and I saw this many times. But the significance of the symbolism at our marriage ceremony became real for me: he had stepped aside and I had taken center stage in her life.

When my children came onto the scene, my family changed again. At this stage it is important to understand that, under normal circumstances, your spousal relationship in the family will outlast the relationships with your children. This is from the point of view that your marriage is designed to last until death, and if your life span is fully lived, your children will usually separate from you and cleave to their spouse in a new familial relationship before you die. So, it is not good to place your relationship with your children ahead of your relationship with your spouse: the marital relationship should come first. It was there before the children, and will be there after the children in the context of family.

The concepts here are delicate so I will insert this idea again. We are talking about primary relationships but not to the exclusion of other relationships. It is incumbent upon us to develop the maturity to know how far to take different relationships without putting the more important relationships in God's design at risk. By no means is it necessary to become islands in isolation from the rest of our wider families or from society. Yet God's design seems to show that good families make good societies, without any evidence that the reverse is true. Given the choice, we need to know where our relative priorities are.

When someone loses his or her spouse it can be a dreadfully lonely journey. There are always other family members, friends and community groups who care. However, I have heard many people who remain behind speak in some way of the hole inside them that other relationships cannot fill. I loved my Mum deeply, but I remember standing by helplessly watching her cry as she told me how lonely she felt for a while after my Dad had passed.

We should never allow our relationship with God to be eclipsed by the relationship with a spouse. I am not, in any way, promoting disharmony of any sort. Perhaps I simply want us to recognize that God must be our first love always. And while we should love our spouse "as Christ loved the church and gave His life for her" (Ephesians 5: 25) in the case of the husband, we must always love God more. Once again we see a reference to the depth of love Christ had for humanity, so much so that He died in order to save us from a life and eternity without a relationship with God. This is the example of the depth of love a husband should have for his wife. Now, we know that people have given their lives for others, or for a cause. Yet even that level of commitment is not to be equated to our commitment to God.

The application of this principle is delicate, especially when two spouses believe different things, so your particular situation needs to be handled according to its unique characteristics. Please don't cut your spouse off under the guise of preserving your relationship with God. Rather, speak to someone who has spiritual oversight in order to work out your specifics.

In summary then we have five general stages of family:

1. The family I am born into
2. The family I create with my spouse
3. The family we create with our children
4. The family with my spouse after my children leave
5. The family I have after my spouse dies

Against this background, we now go to the question, "What do I owe my family?"

What do I Owe My Family as time Evolves?

I was born into a two-parent family; number five of eight siblings. My maternal grandmother lived with us and my paternal grandmother lived with my Dad's youngest sister. I grew up watching how my parents both honored their mothers and I determined at an early age that I would do the same. This flavored my perspective going into adulthood and I will describe shortly how that perspective had to change a little as I better understood the meaning of "honor", as well as the way family changes with time.

My Mum wanted appreciation. She would usually wake up at five o'clock in the morning and prepare a great breakfast of the world's best omelettes for us before we headed off to school. One morning I came into the kitchen and Mum was busy, but she was also "complaining" about things we either had done or hadn't done that she now had to do even though she was so busy. I remember feeling really guilty and I said to her that we didn't need such an elaborate breakfast everyday. We could all make ourselves a sandwich and be fine, and then she could have fewer burdens at the start of each day. My Mum stopped what she was doing and turned to face me. She said that she loved to prepare the breakfast and other things for us; all she wanted was appreciation.

My Dad worked very hard to provide for us, like many other Dads did at that time. I remember once when he decided that he wanted to buy a small trailer for his fishing equipment. This became quite an issue because Mum felt that we didn't have the money for that. But Dad insisted that he wanted to treat himself as well. We had a family meeting as we did frequently, and Dad then decided that he would not get the small trailer after all. His family's immediate needs were more important.

My parents wanted us to be Christian, educated and not secretive. For all that they were doing for me, I felt that these requests were not unreasonable. I determined not to embarrass them by my conduct, to pursue my studies seriously, and to openly share my experiences with them, both good and bad. In sharing, we agreed that if I had to share something controversial, we would relate not as parent to son, but as counselor to client. This was the least I could do to honor them.

Oh how much I've learned since then. I actually thought that I was doing this for them, when in fact the benefit all came back to me. Our open discussions saved me from falling into more pits than I can remember to count. My education has changed the destiny of my family tree. My pursuit of God has saved me from pain in this life and an eternity apart from God.

So you can understand how Exodus 20: 12 (NASB) has become a reality in my life. "Honor your father and your mother, that your days may be prolonged in the land which the Lord your God gives you". This was directly addressed to the nation of Israel, and it concerned their longevity in the land to the west of the Jordan River in the Middle East. But the principle still applies to us today. My attempt to honor my parents has resulted in longevity as measured by the number of blessings God has given to me. That is my experience, in spite of the challenges that every day living has placed before me.

As I have reflected upon my relationships with my siblings, I think that my key contribution to them was encouragement. I can think of many occasions with each of them where I was doing things with the deliberate goal of inspiring them to become something more than they were. I always felt the confidence for them that they were on the verge of some great thing God had for them if they would look to Him.

Before and early during my marriage, I learned the principle that a husband's key role is to make his wife secure. The apostle Paul put it this way: we are to "love our wives as Christ loved the church and gave Himself for it." (Ephesians 5: 25) It took me a while longer to understand what this actually means in every day practical loving.

I had strong feelings about the level of sacrifice we should be willing to bear in order to strengthen our extended family, especially given the blessings we had received from God. What I discovered is that each new family must have its autonomy and privacy to work out their own journey. In this regard, the family needs space and security: spiritual, emotional and material, to determine what that means and is. When they need input, it is up to them to ask for it. When we offer a response, it is exemplary based on biblical models. But each family must be responsible and accountable for their own decisions.

This outlook has freed me up to focus on my immediate family's well being. I talk to my siblings and help them wherever I can, but that takes second place to my wife's needs. If she so much as feels uncomfortable with any interaction or lack of it, that interaction changes and in some cases even stops or starts as required. In a marriage course we took very early in our marital journey, the leaders explained to us that the wife is the spiritual radar. This describes her intuitive sense of spiritual activity, often without any logical explanation, ahead of its manifestation in our natural situation. I don't just believe that now, but I know it to be true in my life.

When the children came along, I slowly came round to understanding my role in bringing security and in being a role model to them. I was particularly exasperated one time when my teen son shared something with me in passing. He had wanted to get a particular haircut and we had strongly counseled him against it. Some Manager at his part-time job told him that he should be able to do what he wants with his hair because "it's his life". Remarkable! This individual had not known my son for even one year, was not paying for his upkeep, had no interest or investment in his future, but offered his opinion freely to an impressionable young person. In my opinion, no one will ever have more interest in our children than we do except their spouse. So I encourage parents to take confidence in the impact of their role and not to allow themselves to feel intimidated by outer influences.

This, of course, is a much broader topic and I think it is worth taking the time to work through your own situation. A parent cannot know everything and therefore there is definitely a need to draw on the wider community in order to inform and position your children for success. Suffice to say that no one has more vested in a child than the parent, so your leadership as they navigate the early years is crucial. Don't delegate that to someone else if at all possible.

This phase is also sometimes the life stage where aging parents need your support. Jesus said that it is evil to withdraw support of your parents with the excuse that you are giving to God's work. (Mark 7: 9 – 13) He said this in the context of people who gave support to religious activities, and used this as an excuse to not provide for the livelihood of their elderly parents. So we understand that it is also our responsibility to care for aging parents.

But it is important to maintain the appropriate balance in doing this. Remember that your first priority is your family, and then your parents. For example, in-laws living with families, commonly known as the sandwich generation, have created challenges that some marriages have not been able to bear. The final state has sometimes been hardship that has far exceeded the hardship of a senior adjusting to life in a long-term care facility. On the other hand, I know some people who willingly embraced this responsibility and were richly blessed in due time. No easy answers are available in this. My best advice is to keep your family's needs as first priority and build solutions around that.

The empty-nest stage in life is an interesting adventure. I am not there yet, but I have friends and colleagues who have arrived and I read of many cases describing peoples' transition into and through this phase. My vision of this period is to give my wife a good life. This is harvest time. I want to spend large amounts of dedicated time together with her doing the things she loves to do.

I plan to enjoy romantic moments, exhilarating adventures and meaningful philanthropy with her.

This will also be the time to concentrate on building on my foundation, an inheritance for my children and grand children. In my view, inheritance is not just money but also heritage. Heritage includes the position or worldview that they take in society and this doesn't just happen, but it must be created. Proverbs 13: 22 (NASB) states that, "a good man leaves an inheritance to his children's children". I understand that this is in the context of the land in Israel. Again, though, I see by extension a principle that is applicable to us today in the matter of what we create for our children.

In the final stage of my family – in this model this means when I am dead and gone – I owe my wife a legacy of dependence upon God. For "Naked I came from my mother's womb, And naked shall I return there." (Job 1: 21). The success of the final stage of my family goes back to the success of my earliest phases of life. As I live with God as my first priority and model that for my wife and children, it sets them up to prosper during their final stages as well. We cannot overestimate the importance of identifying our anchor and then selling out to it totally.

What if you die before all this time line rolls out? Then you sacrifice and die before you enjoy the fruits of your labor, right?

If I die "prematurely" I will have lived well, knowing that I walked faithfully with God and was no more, like Enoch did. (Genesis 5: 24, NIV) It will be good for the servant whose master finds him doing what he was instructed to do.

But if I live out a full life according to God's model both my descendants and me will have the best set up for a happy and prosperous life before the Lord.

Conclusion

This was a loaded chapter for me. When I presented it for the first time before an audience, it generated inner movements that I was not expecting as I spoke about my parents. I had to ask my wife Lucy to read that portion on my behalf.

I want to emphasize once more that this chapter is not about severing relationships; rather, it is about prioritizing them. I think that the most important action step here is for you to return to the family schematic and think through your own situation. You can do it looking both forward and backwards as you try to make sense of how your family relationships have changed and will change with time. Then you may be able to navigate more biblically and effectively through these "oceans where feet may fail". (Oceans, Hillsong United)

CHAPTER 7

HOW MUCH MONEY IS ENOUGH?

But everyone shall sit under his vine and under his
fig tree, And no one shall make them afraid; For
the mouth of the Lord of hosts has spoken.
- Micah 4: 4

No one can serve two masters. Either you will hate the one
and love the other, or you will be devoted to the one and
despise the other. You cannot serve both God and money.
- Matthew 6: 24 (NIV)

Introduction

Chapter 7 "How much Money is Enough?" is intended to do at
least two things: (1) Help us understand how important money is
and (2) Help us decide what amount of money is needed to fund
the first three compartments.

Coming out from my background, I know many people who
had the understanding that it's wrong to be rich. We usually trace
it back to an incorrect interpretation of scriptures like 1 Timothy 6:
10 which states that "the love of money is the root of all evil". The
mistake is to receive this statement as, "*money* is the root of all evil".

I think of money as a medium that stores value. This value motivates people to do what *we* value, so that they can get what *they* value. It is a standard that is accepted in some form by most societies. In fact, Ecclesiastes 10: 19 tells us that "money answers everything". My point here is not to come to any conclusions, but to provoke you to think about the role of money in fulfilling God's mandate for humanity to subdue the earth. What place does money have in getting things done in our society today?

Flowing on from this, the fact that money helps to get things done, comes the next consideration of how much I need to support the things I want to get done during my life. I will use some examples to illustrate how money can be a means to an end. My opinion is that money when taken as the "end", or as your "anchor", has the potential to disappoint deeply. This is why I deliberately place it at number four in the priority listing of the four compartments of the framework for living. But it still does make the cut.

In the final analysis, I think that money should serve me and not the other way around. As you go through this, consider where you would like to stand regarding money, but also where you actually stand right now.

Is Money a "Means" or an "End" for you?

Over time I have had the privilege of asking many people what they would do if they had a million dollars. Overwhelmingly the response across the population over the years has been something to do with how they would spend it. Answers such as "pay off my house", "buy a new car", "take a dream vacation" and "pay off the church mortgage" are some examples.

I remember my vision of what I would do if I had a million dollars. I imagined that I would be a corporate executive and wear a suit and tie to work, drive a flashy car, be important and pull cash out of my wallet anytime there was a need to be met. I realize that this does not directly answer the question, but it is interesting that the response is what would come to my mind in my earlier years. My first response to what I would "do" was about what I would "be". And although this leads to what I would "do", I think I usually thought about money as a means rather than as an end in itself.

Why do we want money? Is it something we want because we simply need to have it? If that is the case, we might prioritize its possession above everything else and measure our life's worth by how much of it we possess. When someone asked Jesus to tell his brother to share their father's inheritance with him, Jesus cautioned that a person's life does not consist of the abundance of things they possess. (Luke 12: 15) I don't think that some people should not have the accumulation of money as their goal. I just think that it's a black hole if there is nothing beyond that. At the very least then, we need to take time to answer the question, "Why do I want money?" and to return to this question occasionally.

What is Money?

One way to get to reasons for wanting money is to think about what it is. What role does money play in our lives and societies?

For some of us, we like to understand where it fits in the overall scheme of things – in other words we really want a macro view. Robert Heilbroner's book "The Worldly Philosophers" gives a perspective on the history of key thinkers in the spheres of trade and economics, and the momentum of their contributions gives us an idea of where the generations might be going.

For others of us, an understanding of the here and now is much more relevant. In this regard, I am not going to try to defend what is the right or wrong approach. In order to deal with life's questions, I simply think that it is important to have some idea of how money works in our world today and to pick an approach to handling what money you are going to have.

The prophet Micah quotes something that is found at least two times earlier in the Bible. He writes about an aspiration where "everyone shall sit under his vine and under his fig tree". (Micah 4: 4) The idea here is that each family would be able to own the means to feed and shelter themselves, taking care of their basic needs for living well. The extension is that there would be no fear of this being taken away by invading armies, so living well is wrapped in both family and societal stability and security.

Jesus says that we will have to choose between serving God and serving money; "No one can serve two masters; for either he will hate the one and love the other, or else he will be loyal to the one and despise the other. You cannot serve God and mammon". (Matthew 6: 24) For those in our society who don't believe in God, the choice about money is equally applicable. Will you serve money or not? The evidence I see is that no one can predict what will happen to him or her financially. The element of fate is the unknown that gives two people who do the same things different results.

A small example might illustrate the point. Many people today believe in and are working towards receiving a defined benefit pension, where they contribute to a fund and expect to receive a guaranteed percentage of their current income adjusted for inflation until they die (simply stated). My Dad had such a pension. It worked for a while but ended up being worth virtually nothing due to external factors. Does this mean that defined benefit pensions are bad? No, I think many would agree that they are a good idea. In fact, many people from my Dad's generation in other parts of the world currently benefit from these pensions. However, the opportunity cost is high and the result is not guaranteed.

I think there are at least two approaches to Jesus' statement about serving money.

Some people decide that they will not serve money so they *plan* to do without many things that money can buy, and accept that they will be largely *dependent* upon those who have money for some of their wider needs. Mother Theresa was a great example of this. When she received her Nobel Peace Prize, she asked that the presentation dinner be cancelled and the money used to support the work she was doing within the poor community. She did not serve money, and turned her back on some of the pleasures it could bring, but was dependent on those who had money in order to be effective in her work.

Other people *plan* to be basically financially *independent* so that they don't serve money. They work to set themselves up so that they don't rely directly on others to give them money for what they need or even what they want. In this sense, they do not serve money. Rather, money serves them. There are two models I have learned that come at this from slightly different points of view.

Robert Kiyosaki (an American investor, entrepreneur, self-help author, motivational speaker, financial literacy activist, and financial commentator) says that money is an idea. How you think about it determines what you choose to do. His book "Rich Dad, Poor Dad" explains why it is important to acquire as many assets as you can (things that generate ongoing income for you), and as few liabilities as you need (things that generate ongoing expenses for you). His message is basically that you need to move to being a business owner or investor as quickly as possible, where you don't have to exert your time and effort in order to get income. Robert and his wife left their jobs and were homeless for a few weeks as they struggled to set up assets that have since released him to pursue his teaching passion.

Dave Ramsay, a well-known American Christian financial expert, has built a seven-step model based on biblical principles that some people think is more accessible to the less entrepreneurial. It offers a way that even with a job, people with focus can become debt free and build up reserves that leave them less dependent on outside sources for their livelihood and retirement. Dave was a millionaire in his twenties and then went bankrupt due to debt. He is now debt free, wealthy and does what he enjoys – helping others to emulate his pattern.

Again, I am not making any assessments on which models are right or wrong. But I do stress the need to educate yourself about money, pick an approach and then work it. Let me describe the way I approach the funding of my life priorities.

Funding the Compartments

When I visited India in 2014, our host was explaining the caste system to me. The simple understanding I have is that the caste system is a form of hierarchical social segmentation, or class ranking. Of significance for our purpose, the caste at the top of the hierarchy is not those who are necessarily rich, but those whose families have done significant things for the community over time. The merchant caste is at a lower level. This certainly resonates with my perspective that life has more than simply money as a priority and is perhaps best lived when we improve the quality of life for other people.

After an enduring personal relationship with God, my priorities are to establish a strong family, and then to make a significant impact in my generation to peoples' mental and material quality of life. This requires at least two things: I must be in good shape personally in order to do what I need to do over time, and I'll need money to make this happen in the world that we live in. The question is how much money do I need and how am I getting it?

In my case and with the goals I have for my family, I have a plan to be basically independent. By this I mean that I need to have enough invested so that I have income to take care of my family's basic needs. I understand how much money that is per month, and how much I need to put aside for things that come up in the longer term such as replacement vehicles. I also have an idea of how much we will need in retirement for a basic but comfortable life. With this understanding, I am on a quest to get our finances in order.

Lucy and I are both workers and we are not afraid to put effort and commitment into things we believe in. I think this would be true of the average citizen in the city we live in. Thus, I knew that Lucy was capable of delayed gratification, as long as it was delayed and not denied. However, time is never on your side. I wanted my children to grow up in a comfortable and spacious home, and in a neighborhood that was not crowded but also close to the action of city life. While I wanted to instill in them the ethos of work and its relationship to reward, I also wanted them to be exposed to some of the fine things in life at an early age. My son Daniel got a taste of this while we were in Zimbabwe, where he lived for a little under two years.

By the time I came to Canada and started over again, I understood that making the money of a corporate executive didn't necessarily make me wealthy. Getting a passive income that would free up my time to do what I wanted to do seemed more appealing. So I tried to start a business and later to start a consulting practice. Each time, for whatever reason, the enterprise didn't succeed as I needed it to and I went back to chasing the corporate ladder in order to stay on track with my life goals. The beauty for me then is that I have settled on the investment I have made in myself through education and corporate experience to bring me to the financial targets I have set.

I have volunteered in the church practically all my life in order to help people, and done so with increasing intensity. Let me insert here that I receive more help in the process of helping others, than I actually probably give. Through my Rotary Ambassadorial Scholar experience and my exposure to international work through the church, I have come to understand how relatively little money is needed to impact peoples' lives abroad, and how willing people in North America are to support this as long as there is demonstrated credibility. I have an experienced view of how financial freedom for me can open opportunities to make a difference in areas I care deeply about. Therefore, let's descend rapidly to where the rubber meets the road.

Lucy and I have worked off a family budget for many years. We always target the following: taxes are taken first, we give 10% of gross income to the church, at least 1% to philanthropy, live within what remains, apply bonuses to debt reduction and retirement savings. Regardless of the income, this has always been a struggle; one that I don't think will end because it continues to teach us to have financial discipline. We give up several times a year but always come back to base. What I've learned is that if I don't know where the money is going, I'll never plug the drains.

In a society that values you based on your position, having as capable a person as Lucy out of formal employment for some of her time in Canada has been difficult. With employment comes a sense of belonging as you contribute to society in a way that society visibly values. But I have seen two great benefits of this: the first is that Lucy has been able to dedicate the time that I think is biblically modeled for raising of children; and the second is that she has been freed up to be available to set up for life mission critical things we want to do.

Our level of income has been adequate to live a very comfortable life...if we were prepared to remain in debt. Using Dave Ramsay's guidelines, however, we wanted to eliminate debt as quickly as possible. So we have sacrificed but in relatively smart ways.

Vacations and exposure for our family have been very strategic for us. We have not always taken the vacations we wanted to *when* we wanted to but our children have been abroad and have seen sites and stayed at venues that are some of the best in the world. We often got excited along with those from all over the world who spend tons of money every year to come to Toronto. We didn't have to pay what they were paying in order to enjoy what they were enjoying. Our kids especially enjoyed the culture days we would have during summer vacations where we would choose a culture for each day of the week, research that culture, visit cultural sites, eat the food and then have a family discussion about the lessons learned.

The children have participated in extracurricular activity to the extent of their commitment. Music would be an example of this. As long as they were interested in learning and dedicating time and energy to it, we were interested in paying tuition and taking them to classes. When they lost interest, we lost interest too, and the funding was cut.

We are as committed to their education as they are. Our arrangement is that we will pay for their first degrees within Toronto. Anything beyond this will be based on our assessment of the value of what they want to do. We believe that a first degree provides a strong basic level of education from which they can launch into independent life. However, we also find great meaning by investing in causes we believe in. Therefore, to the extent that we see their chosen post-graduate education as a good investment, we will certainly support them based on need. Yet the case would need to be compelling, as it would stand against the resource requirements of some of our life goals.

These are some examples of the way our family has managed our finances. An overarching goal was to follow Dave Ramsay's model and pay off our mortgage within fifteen years. Remarkably, this is on track to happen and it is due to some of the disciplines I've described. All things being equal, this will release the type of cash flow we need to make inroads into our ministry work without putting the family's wellbeing at risk. At the same time, we can seriously focus on our retirement years and building up an inheritance for the next generation.

Conclusion

I am not about to suggest that what I have described in this chapter is the best financial approach. I couldn't in all seriousness suggest such a thing when so many people have become eminently more successful than me financially, and in a much shorter period of time. But I do want to re-focus and return to the objective of this text. I am trying to give you a framework for dealing with life's questions while you are living through these things. For me, researching and choosing an approach to deal with my finances in a meaningful way that relates to my life purpose is helping when curved balls hit me along the way. To the extent that this helps you to chart your own frame that will be helpful, I shall be glad.

I recognize that this chapter has a primarily cognitive or technical focus. While my leaning is towards highlighting the fact that God has given us the ability to learn skills that will make us more capable of being successful with money, I do need to mention the spiritual dimensions of this subject. Many people have stories about how they have been blessed with money in ways that they can only describe as miraculous. There are also distinct principles of faith giving in the Bible that defy human logic and accentuate the reality of spiritual laws that reward this type of giving. Suffice to say that I have personally experienced such blessings in my life, but I will leave the topic to others with more dedicated writings on biblical finance.

Now we come to your actions. Do you have financial goals and a plan? I know…many times we have goals and then lose heart because it looks impossible. I want to encourage you, have a huge dream, and then break it down so that you can see what the essential first step is that would give you independence and work towards that. The journey of a thousand miles begins with the first step, according to an old Chinese proverb.

Figure out what it costs to do things you value in your life. Break them down into needs and wants. Tackle the needs first, and once that is fully covered, tackle the wants. The best way to know what is necessary is to find someone who has what you want, gain his or her interest in you and learn what it takes from the inside. This way you have a credible understanding of what is required. But you first need to know what you want. That way, you won't end up like I did; finding out that being a corporate executive didn't quite meet what I was looking for to enable my needs and life mission.

If you choose Mother Theresa's path and decide to not pursue money for yourself and to forego many of the things that money can buy, that can be a great decision. My opinion is simply that you should then not find fault with those who choose to make and use money to meet their life missions, and also that you should not feel entitled to receive the fruits of what others have gained. From afar it seems to me that this is one way that Mother Theresa honored God and in so doing became honorable herself.

As a final thought, I want to return to a consideration from chapter 6. What if you die before all this time line rolls out? Then you sacrifice and die before you enjoy the fruits of your labor right?

If I die "prematurely" I will have lived well, knowing that I walked faithfully with God and was no more, like Enoch did. (Genesis 5: 24, NIV) It will be good for the servant whose master finds him doing what he was instructed to do.

But if I live out a full life according to God's model, not only will I keep my mind, but also both my descendants and me will have the best set up for a happy and prosperous life before the Lord.

EPILOGUE

We arrive at the Epilogue, the conclusion of this reflection. Again, I must acknowledge that, "there is nothing new under the sun". (Ecclesiastes 1: 9) This is how I apply the quotation: I have written this text out of my experience, but my experience and perspective have been enriched by countless readings, talks and leaders, most of whom I cannot remember specifically in order to attribute. Therefore, *I claim nothing original in this work*, and I will now give a survey of samples of other material that will serve you well as you choose to pay attention to keeping your mind by dealing with life's questions in your lifetime.

At the end of Chapter 5 I promised to return to the question of time: where do I find the time for myself in order to accomplish all that has been placed in my heart to accomplish? I want to now give some thought to the subjects of balance and scheduling. Some personalities will handle these in a very precise way, while others will be much more intuitive. Either way, I do believe that if you do not get a grip of this, you are at risk of not meeting your potential.

Write down and etch into your memory the things that are most important to you. Return to these things frequently. Block out time in your day, week, month and year, that you dedicate to these few things that you have determined to be most important. Then do not break these blocks lightly for something else, and never break them before finding another block of time to keep your commitment to yourself.

Eight to nine o'clock three times a week in the gym instead of in front of the TV could prolong the quality of your health without any notable time impact.

Thirty minutes of reflection every morning could reset your compass and tap into an enthusiastic mindset without any notable time impact.

Thinking about your paycheck before you spend your hard earned money can save you years of debt without any notable impact to your quality of life.

Having a twenty minute meal with your family everyday will keep you in touch and potentially save you a lifetime of remedial work in later years.

Kissing your spouse goodbye and hello everyday could save you the heavy price in time and money of a later separation, without any notable time impact.

I could go on, but I do pray that you get the picture. You can build small disciplines into your routine to use time that is currently being wasted, for your intended aspirations without much more effort than you are already making.

And now as you go forward, in the words of Numbers 6: 24 – 26 (NLT):

May the Lord bless you and protect you.
May the Lord smile on you and be gracious to you.
May the Lord show you his favor and give you his peace.

A SELECTED BIBLIOGRAPHY

Chapter 1 "Find an Anchor for the Mind"

1. Play the song "Oceans" by Hillsong United as you read these words:

You call me out upon the waters, the great unknown, where feet may fail. And there I find You in the mystery; in oceans deep my faith will stand.

And I will call upon Your name, and keep my eyes above the waves when oceans rise.
My soul will rest in Your embrace, for I am Yours and You are mine.

Your grace abounds in deepest waters. Your sovereign hand will be my guide where feet may fail and fear surrounds me. You've never failed and You won't start now.

So I will call upon Your name, and keep my eyes above the waves when oceans rise.
My soul will rest in Your embrace, for I am Yours and You are mine.

Spirit lead me where my trust is without borders
Let me walk upon the waters wherever You would call me
Take me deeper than my feet could ever wander
And my faith will be made stronger in the presence of my Savior

2. Read the Book of Ecclesiastes from the Bible in one sitting.

The book is written as an autobiography telling of King Solomon's investigation of the meaning of life and how best to live. He says that everything we do is inherently vain or meaningless because the lives of both wise and foolish people end in death. To live well on earth, Solomon endorses wisdom. However, his internal debate laid out in this writing draws no correlation between living wisely and eternal consequence. Therefore, if the end of all people is the same, it does not make sense to focus on all the stresses of life. Rather, he proposes that it is important to enjoy the simple pleasures of daily life, such as eating, drinking, and taking enjoyment in one's work, which are gifts from God. But he concludes with the injunction: "Fear God, and keep his commandments; for that is the whole duty of everyone"

3. The Confessions of Saint Augustine, by Saint Augustine of Hippo

This book outlines Augustine's sinful youth and his conversion to Christianity. Written as an autobiography around the turn of the fifth century AD it is still widely read in seminaries and philosophy schools. Therefore, the book has had a significant influence on Christianity and more generally on Western Civilization.

Augustine wrote this book in his early forties so it is not a complete account of his life experiences. However, his documented thought processes grapple with many issues common to human beings. It is a significant theological work and it presents many spiritual meditations and insights. It was required reading for several courses on my Master of Divinity Program.

In the work St. Augustine writes about how much he regrets having led a sinful and immoral life. He spans not only physical but also intellectual and spiritual immorality, and discusses his regrets for following the Manichaean, religion and believing in astrology. Nebridius is a man who helped to persuade him that astrology was not only incorrect but also evil, and St. Ambrose played a part in his conversion to Christianity. So the influences of key figures in Augustine's life are well described in the book.

The first nine books are autobiographical and the last four are commentary. Augustine shows intense sorrow for his sexual sins, and writes on the importance of sexual morality. The books were written as prayers to God, thus the title, based on the Psalms of David; and it begins with "For Thou hast made us for Thyself and our hearts are restless till they rest in Thee."

I recommend this reading because it is written from the heart. Its words capture even subconscious movements in remarkably perceptive realizations about how people really are. Most importantly, Augustine finds his anchor. This is a detailed, personal and close up insight into the way that a clearly impactful person thought about life. It was a great help to me.

Chapter 2 "Find a Purpose for your Life"

1.   Maslow's Hierarchy of Needs (Abraham Maslow)

This is a theory that describes human motivation. While it has attracted criticism, I find it useful as a reference framework. The development progresses from Physiological upwards to Self Actualization. A description of basic human needs is as follows:

- *Physiological:* Peoples' first motivation is to have our physical needs such as air, water and food met.
- *Safety:* Our next motivation is to secure our personal needs such as health, assets and dependents.

- *Love / Belonging:* Then comes the need for interpersonal fulfillment through relationships with spouse, family and friends.
- *Esteem:* From these bases we reach out towards a type of independence that desires respect both from self and others.
- *Self-Actualization:* At this level people are motivated to become the best that we can be, driven by attributes we recognize within ourselves.

Maslow suggested that these are not sequential milestones but that there is some amount of overlap based on different life circumstances.

2. Holy Discontent (Bill Hybels)

In this book Bill Hybels seeks to address the question, "What comes before vision?" If you are frustrated with some aspect of this broken world, that is likely a reflection of your holy discontent. When you allow yourself to be fueled rather than frustrated by this holy discontent, you get the energy to fulfill your role in making what's wrong in this world right.

3. The Service Profit Chain (JL Heskett, WE Sasser, LA Schlesinger)

This book presents the theory that it is loyal employees who make loyal customers, and loyal customers result in profitable growth. Heskett and Sasser also ran a course at Harvard Business School that covers this content. The content is detailed and conceptually rigorous but you can also extract the key messages without having to internalize all the detail. More than one successful company has grafted this model into their mission statement.

Chapter 3 "Find a Framework to Guide your Living"

1. You Inc (Burke Hedges)

   The key to balancing your life is to allot equal amounts of time and attention to each of the Five F's. Here they are in the order of their importance.

   I.   Faith.
   II. Family.
   III. Fitness.
   IV. Friends.
   V.   Finances.

To better explain how the Five F's affect the balance in your life, think of balance as a wheel. In the center of the wheel is a hub called Faith. The spokes connecting the hub to the rim of the wheel would be the other four F's — that is, Family ... Fitness ... Friends ... and Finances.

2. The Seven Habits of Highly Effective People (Stephen Covey)

Independence

The First Three Habits are about self-mastery. They are about moving from dependence to independence:

1. Be Proactive
    Take charge and be responsible for your roles and relationships in life.

2. Begin with the End in Mind

Be clear in your own mind about what you want to accomplish in the future so that you know with strong definition what it is that you want to make a reality.

3. Put First Things First
   This habit is about disciplining oneself to do the things that are most important in getting to the desired end state; this is called "prioritization" of things to be done.

Interdependence

The next three habits talk about Interdependence or the need to complement one another:

4. Think Win-Win
   Cultivate genuine feelings for mutually beneficial solutions or agreements in relationships. The underlying philosophy is that life does not have to be a zero sum game, meaning that for every winner there must be a loser. Rather, it can be a positive sum game where a "win" for everyone is a better resolution in the long term because all parties feel "whole" and not cheated.

5. Seek First to Understand, Then to be Understood
   It is important to listen to others without preconceptions and to use empathy in genuinely trying to see the subject from their point of view. There is then a good chance that the other person will take the time to try to understand your own position. Such reciprocation leads to a caring atmosphere, which then lends itself to positive problem solving.

6. Synergize

    This is the principle where the whole becomes more than the sum of the individual parts. Positive teamwork results in outcomes that no individual team member could have achieved alone.

Continuous Improvements

The final habit is that of continuous improvement in both the personal and interpersonal spheres of influence.

7. Sharpen the Saw

    Learning, practice and preparation are continuing disciplines for those who want to remain highly effective. For sustained success over the long term, resources, energy and health must be frequently assessed and topped up.

3. All The World's A Stage, William Shakespeare's As You Like It, Act II, Scene VII

Jaques to Duke Senior:
All the world's a stage,
And all the men and women merely players;
They have their exits and their entrances,
And one man in his time plays many parts,
His acts being seven ages. At first, the infant,
Mewling and puking in the nurse's arms.
Then the whining schoolboy, with his satchel
And shining morning face, creeping like snail
Unwillingly to school. And then the lover,
Sighing like furnace, with a woeful ballad
Made to his mistress' eyebrow. Then a soldier,
Full of strange oaths and bearded like the pard,

Jealous in honour, sudden and quick in quarrel,
Seeking the bubble reputation
Even in the canon's mouth. And then the justice,
In fair round belly with good capon lined,
With eyes severe and beard of formal cut,
Full of wise saws and modern instances;
And so he plays his part. The sixth age shifts
Into the lean and slippered pantaloon
With spectacles on nose and pouch on side;
His youthful hose, well saved, a world too wide
For his shrunk shank, and his big manly voice,
Turning again toward childish treble, pipes
And whistles in his sound. Last scene of all,
That ends this strange eventful history,
Is second childishness and mere oblivion,
Sans teeth, sans eyes, sans taste, sans everything.
(As You Like It, 2. 7. 139-167)

Chapter 4 "What does God want from Me?"

1. The Purpose Driven Life (Rick Warren)

The most basic question everyone faces in life is, "Why am I here? What is my purpose?" Warren explains God's five purposes for us:

I.   We were planned for God's pleasure so your first purpose is to offer real worship.
II. We were formed for God's family so your second purpose is to enjoy real fellowship.
III. We were created to become like Christ, so your third purpose is to learn real discipleship.

IV. We were shaped for serving God so your fourth purpose is to practice real ministry.

V. We were made for a mission so your fifth purpose is to live out real evangelism.

2. Holy Listening: The Art of Spiritual Direction (Margaret Guenther)

This is one of several texts of its kind where the spiritual director helps the directee to hear the voice of God in the various elements of her life. Guenther uses stories of real people to bring this discipline to life.

3. Gandhi An Autobiography: The Story of My Experiments with truth (Mohandas Karamchand Gandhi)

Mohandas K. Gandhi, in this classic autobiography, tells the story of his life and how he developed his concept of active nonviolent resistance. This approach propelled the Indian struggle for independence, and also provided the blue print for many other nonviolent struggles during the twentieth century. Ghandi describes periods of tremendous disappointment. Yet his choice to open up his inner thoughts and feelings to us show cases the power of conviction especially when faced with overwhelming let downs that can easily be called failures. At the very least, this work's inspiration lies in the revelation that even revered leaders must figure life out in an attempt to "keep their minds". So, if *they* aren't spared this challenge, we are in good company.

Chapter 5 "Selfless or Selfish?"

1. Leading on Empty: Refilling Your Tank and Renewing Your Passion (Wayne Cordeiro)

Wayne tells the story of how he found himself paralyzed by burnout. He had been in ministry for thirty years, and burnout came ten years after founding what is now the largest church in Hawaii. He took a season out of his growing ministry to recharge and refocus on what was truly important to him. In his case, this involved checking into a monastery and withdrawing all contact with electronic and other forms of media. It meant getting back in touch with his life and regaining proper balance. It re-energized his spirit through Christ and he came back to serve with new passion and joy.

2. Good to Great (Jim Collins)

This is the outcome of a research study from which Jim and his team addressed the question of why some companies make the leap from good to great, sustained performance. He begins with the statement that "good is the enemy of great" and describes seven characteristics of companies that went from good to great.

- Level 5 Leadership: Leaders who are humble, but driven to do what's best for the company.
- First Who, Then What: Get the right people on the bus, then figure out where to go. Try the right people out in different positions in order to find the best fit.
- Confront the Brutal Facts: The Stockdale paradox – confront the brutal truth of the situation yet at the same time, never give up hope.
- Hedgehog Concept: Three overlapping circles: What lights your fire ("passion")? What could you be best in the world at ("best at")? What makes you money ("driving resource")?
- Culture of Discipline: Rinsing the cottage cheese. The example here is of a triathlete who literally rinsed his

cottage cheese to get rid of excess fat from his diet and it speaks to the advantage of above – average discipline.

- Technology Accelerators: Using technology to accelerate growth, within the three circles of the hedgehog concept.
- The Flywheel: The additive effect of many small initiatives; they act on each other like compound interest.

3. The Art of War (Sun Tzu)

Sun Tzu considered war as a necessary evil that must be avoided whenever possible. It should be fought swiftly to avoid economic losses. He emphasized the importance of positioning in military strategy. The decision to position an army must be based on both objective conditions in the physical environment and the subjective beliefs of other, competitive factors in that environment. Planning works in a controlled environment; but in a changing environment, competing plans collide creating unexpected situations that must be handled.

This book helped me to identify what I don't want to be, while making me aware of some of the thinking in my environment.

Chapter 6 "What do I Owe my Family?"

1. Focus on the Family (Founder James Dobson)

Mission: nurturing and defending the God-ordained institution of the family and promoting biblical truths worldwide. Website: www.focusonthefamily.ca

Chapter 7 "How much Money is Enough?"

1. The Worldly Philosophers: The Lives, Times and Ideas of the Great Economic Thinkers (Robert Heilbroner)

This book examines the history of economic thought from Adam Smith to Karl Marx. It enables us to see more deeply into our history and also helps us better understand our own times. At its core this work outlines various attempts to understand capitalism. Schools of thought range from purely scientific to spheres that include political and social dimensions. For us, this is a mere peep into the debates of thought leaders that have framed the world we live in. The better we understand this world, the better positioned we are to make effective decisions for our personal lives.

2. Rich Dad Poor Dad (Robert Kiyosaki)

This book highlights the different attitudes to money, work and life of two men and how they influenced key decisions in Kiyosaki's life. "Rich Dad" was in fact Kiyosaki's friend's Dad who used defined principles to build a very wealthy estate. "Poor Dad" was Kiyosaki's biological Dad who was a professional who lost his job and did not achieve financial success. A key concern is personal financial literacy, which he feels is woefully inadequate in the general population.

Some topics the book deals with include:

- The definition of assets (purchases that produce net cash inflows) and liabilities (purchases that produce net cash outflows).
- What the rich, middle class and poor teach their kids about money
- The importance of financial intelligence literacy

3. The Total Money Makeover: A Proven Plan for Financial Fitness by Dave Ramsey

Getting out of debt will not happen overnight; it takes time. Here are the baby steps that will get you started:

Step 1: $1,000 to start an Emergency Fund
Step 2 Pay off all debt with the Debt Snowball
Step 3: 3 to 6 months' expenses in savings
Step 4: Invest 15% of income into Pre-Tax Retirement Plans
Step 5: College funding for children
Step 6: Pay off your home early
Step 7: Build wealth and give!

Adrian Peel
May 2015

ACKNOWLEDGEMENTS

Life matters and because it does, our response to the vicissitudes of life also matter. I have had the privilege of spending quality time with many people from different backgrounds in different parts of the world. I'd like to thank all the people with whom I've had interactions regarding this subject, for your immense contribution and support in seeing me through this book.

I would like to specifically express my gratitude to Granville McKenzie, Trevor Rajah, Louis O'Brien and Patrice White who read through this book and offered insightful comments that assisted me in clarifying my thoughts. A special thank you to my brother Gareth Peel who inspired me to write this book, and also offered a comprehensive review.

I would also like to thank my wife, Lucy, who knows me better than anyone else, for her love, support and encouragement during this process. Doing life with her has helped me "keep my mind" through rough and unchartered situational terrain. To my children, Daniel and Andrea, who have taught me so much, "Thank you".

Finally, I want to thank God for the gift He has given me, as well as for the opportunity to reach out and to touch His people in this capacity. I am thankful for His incredible grace and mercy that has kept me throughout this course. Thank you Lord.

ENDNOTES

1. "Pigs don't know pigs stink", Amway Tape
2. Proverbs 23: 7
3. 1 Timothy 6: 10
4. Ecclesiastes 1: 9
5. Drawn by Patrice White, Toronto, Canada
6. "We Have An Anchor", Traditional Hymn, Priscilla Jane Owens
7. Matthew 25: 21
8. Maslow, A.H. (1943). A theory of human motivation. Psychological Review 50 (4) 370–96. https://commons.wikimedia.org/wiki/File:Maslow%27s_hierarchy_of_needs.svg
9. Gonzalez, Justo L. "The Story of Christianity Volume 2", pp 28, HarperSanFrancisco
10. The Ugly Duckling, Hans Christian Andersen
11. http://healthysleep.med.harvard.edu
12. "Theme from Mahogany (Do You Know Where You're Going To)"

CPSIA information can be obtained
at www.ICGtesting.com
Printed in the USA
LVOW12*1107060416

482418LV00006B/18/P

9 781512 734867